# Endorsements

"*The Missing Moved In* is an exquisitely written, heart-wrenching, gorgeously honest memoir of grief and loss, and the pain with which they leave us. While it is a story of grief and loss, it is also a story of faith, hope and love. Laura's love for her father, as well as her longing to trust in God, pulses on every page. This tender and touching book is one of the best books on grief and loss I have read. I read it in one sitting because I could not put it down."

~James Bryan Smith
author of *The Good and Beautiful God*

"With touching empathy and genuine transparency, Laura Fox's book *The Missing Moved In: A Grief Journey* speaks powerfully of the pain connected with the loss of a treasured loved one, her extraordinary father, and my dear friend of many years, Fred Stoesz, an urban missionary and church planter. Laura's account weaves a touching depiction of Fred's character, relationships, and family from a caring and yet grieving daughter's point of view. She recounts Fred's unique story with grace and skill, honestly testifying to what it means to face the numbing reality of such a devastating loss while maintaining both true meaning and hope. Laura's poignant memoir is much more than a mere witness of personal loss. Everyone who reads this sensitive and powerful portrayal of their family's struggle with the loss of Fred's life will learn much about what it means to face the darkest depths of such unthinkable grief courageously with grace and tenderness.

After reading Laura's book I believe it offers graduate-level heart insight in what it means to grieve well. Her account will equip the reader with how to embrace both the honor of a life lived well and the unthrottled pain of the 'Missing,' spoken in her own words, 'find solace in my journey that might somewhat mirror your own.' This book is essential for anyone seeking to remember the uniqueness of an extraordinary life like Fred's, so profoundly shared in love, and yet also learn to persevere and be healed from the irreplaceable loss of someone like him, a gifted husband, brother, dad, and friend."

~Rev. Dr. Don L. Davis
Sr. Vice President, World Impact; Executive Director, TUMI

"If music is said to be the universal language of mankind, then grief is its unchained melody in a hauntingly beautiful minor key. *The Missing Moved In* is a familiar refrain recognized by those who have navigated the aftermath of loss, regardless of its source. Laura gently holds the hands and hearts of her readers and normalizes the whisperings they hear repeatedly through blurred lines of sorrowful prayers and reality. What she offers is atypical - a permission to feel and to stay. A call to lessen the hurrying up of grief even though the call to 'heal' is so strong in our circles of support. Fox intimately invites the reader to lay down their boxing gloves - to bear witness to the Missing in their lives and to bear witness to the beauty around them. I highly recommend this book as both a means of lament and salve for grieving hearts."

~Quantrilla Ard
author, Founder of 'Its All Grief to Me' Podcast

"With poetic grace, Laura Fox carries readers on a journey of grief, lament, loneliness, fear, and hope. Her vulnerability is a welcome place for an honest look at the echoes of longing. Her words are both convicting and comforting—and her story is one for everyone who has had loss written into theirs."

~Ronne Rock
mentor, speaker, and author of *One Woman Can Change the World: Reclaiming Your God-Designed Influence and Impact Right Where You Are*

"Laura's vulnerability invites us all into the deeper waters of unknown grief. Without the promise of a better future, she explores the enormity of loss through beautiful language, offering the reader a chance to wander through their own story with a new intentionality and curiosity. May we all find the courage to grieve with such intention and hope."

~Mandy Capehart
author & trauma-informed grief educator

"Reflecting on an intimate season of family loss, *The Missing Moved In* serves as a faithful companion for wading through grief. From rich life experiences as a pastor's daughter, military spouse, and young mother, storyteller Laura Fox takes a brave seat on the pew beside fellow mourners, offering gentle sips of solace and hope."

~Peyton H. Roberts
author of *Beneath the Seams*

"*The Missing Moved In* was a heartbreakingly raw read, and yet I couldn't pull myself away from Laura's eloquent and honest assessment of grief. The way she crafts stories and meaning to them, and clings to a battered faith in the midst of heartache and transition, had me looking inward and noticing all the stripped bare places grief has touched my own life. The experience of Laura's grief and the poignant way she transcribes such agony stayed with me for days, as her grief, and as my own. A must-read for those wrestling with the *why's* in loss, for anyone ready to settle down with their grief and make peace with its presence. This book helped me do that."

~Eden Campbell
published poet, and writer

"With captivating honesty, Laura opens to us this window into both the beauty and the raw lament of her love for her dad, a love that burns on even years after his passing. In faithfully journeying beside both God and her family through the darkest nights, Laura has been entrusted with a uniquely tender wisdom, which she now offers to us, wrapped in the stories within these pages. Laura's easy companionship and writing style make *The Missing Moved* In a profound gift to anyone trying to find their footing in a disorienting season of grief. I am so grateful for her work."

~Dana Butler
writer, artist, worship leader, grieving daughter

# THE MISSING MOVED IN
**A Grief Journey**

# THE MISSING MOVED IN
## A Grief Journey

LAURA FOX

LUCIDBOOKS

for my abba.

# Table of Contents

# FOREWORD

There is a long and rich tradition among writers of Christian literature who probe deeply and artfully into their emotions, questions, and pain associated with their journey of grief and loss and, in doing so, offer we their readers messages of hope and healing for our own seasons of anguish.

The examples are numerous, and the impact profound.

Writing under the penname N.W. Clerk after the death of his beloved wife Joy Davidman, C.S. Lewis gave us one such rich meditation in his book *A Grief Observed*. It's a book that many readers have turned to again and again as they have faced the death of a loved one and grappled with the accompanying question, *"Why?"* I am among their number.

The former United Nations General Secretary Dag Hammarskjöld's enduring spiritual classic *Markings*, published posthumously two years after Lewis's work, is another example, a book I return to each year for sustenance in bite-sized clusters of words borne out of a very deep and tender place in the life of this Swedish statesmen.

In more recent days, books like Nancy Guthrie's *Holding On to Hope,* Gerald Sittser's *A Grace Disguised* and Nicholas Wolterstorff's *Lament for a Son* have chronicled loss through carefully-crafted stories that neither minimize the authors' loss and pain nor leave those who encounter them without a sense of our ability to overcome by the grace of a God who loves us and cares for us in our own seasons of grief.

And now, with the publication of *The Missing Moved In,* I have another treasure I will be reading and recommending for years to come as find myself – or my family or a friend - in need of a reminder of the ever-present Light even in the midst of darkness. The book you hold in your hands is written by a newer, younger, but no less wise voice, Laura Fox. Her book, like those mentioned above, is borne out of a tender place tended to through careful reflection and a heart open to the work of God, to the love of God, to the hope found in Christian community.

In these pages, you will encounter a lyrical portrait of one woman's wrestling through a paradoxical season of immense loss and joyful new life. Her words offer vivid detail as she seeks to draw us not only into *her* story but into our own stories where maybe, just maybe, we have a similar space of loss, of darkness in need of light and life.

"There's always something to miss – to long for. To look back on and wish we'd really taken it in when we were in it," Laura writes in the latter pages of this book. "Yet, the longer I live with the persistent missing, the more I grow to understand: The Missing will only be at rest when it is found in the presence of Abba. An Abba that never leaves nor forsakes."

Ultimately, that is what *The Missing Moved In* does: It leads us as Laura's readers to a recognition of the goodness and presence of

One who is always with us, even on those days when the winds whip across plains, when the violent storms kick up their heels, when the skies seem darkened with clouds, and we brace ourselves for what is to come.

And we know, even then, we are not alone.

Join me in reading this remarkable book. Join me in taking in the vibrant images it paints with a textured palette of words borne out of the heart, soul and strength of a woman who has paid attention to the contours of her life, and who has chosen yet sing, to open her mouth (and use her pen) to bring beauty to the world.

**Jeff Crosby**, author of
*The Language of the Soul: Meeting God in the Longings of Our Hearts*

# INTRODUCTION

To the robbed.
To the gutted and numb.

To those who avoid the greeting card aisle, and get sick at the scent of lilies.
To those for whom an empty chair is not a vacant seat.
To those who press on in the after, stuffing pockets full of holes with memories of the before.

You, who have held the cold weight of ashes in your hands not known where or how to set them down. Or stood beside broken earth willing yourself not to fall in too.

To those who carry the feverish skin of the dying in the archives of your fingertips, and whose voice once whispered a feeble "it's okay" when it wasn't.

It wasn't okay.

To the walking legacies limping after new traditions.

You, who hides your tears in closets and showers because you're supposed to be "over it."

You, who's been pulled up by the roots and told to grow.

To those who remember when trust came easier, and hope wasn't so slippery.

To those who dare ask the questions, and have allowed doubt to have a place at grace's table.

To those who live with the Missing.
Read and know—
*you are seen.*

Laura

# CHAPTER 1

# Glimpses of the Missing

*The day the Missing moved in, it tried to kill me.*
*I saw it coming like a storm cloud. I watched its approach—*
*ominous and slow.*
*I had known it would arrive, and yet, still it took me by violent*
*surprise. The force of it rushed around me with a deafening roar. It*
*swept me up as if I were nothing, as if I had no mass or feelings or*
*soul. I couldn't tell which way was up and which was down.*
*My reality collided with it as if it were a brick wall—breaking me.*

I'm a Kansas girl.

I know the scent of tornados.

Prairie girls have charcoal clouds in their eyes. We know the color of destruction. We've seen it moving steadily across the fields: summer wheat bowing in golden worship to the clouds which have merged into a solid wall of darkness.

Our noses have been trained to tell the difference between a normal Great Plains thunderstorm and one that will give birth to twisters hungry for demolition.

The wind carries with it a warning. It travels up our nostrils bringing with it an aromatic mixture of grass, asphalt, and alfalfa with notes of metal—that's when we know. Danger approaches.

Hair in hand and feet planted in a steadying wide stance, we squint into the wind. We can identify at which shade of deepening indigo gray the clouds will begin to produce more than hail. We know when we must seek shelter—burrow as deep into the ground as we can. Deep among the roots.

We wait in the dark, ears peeled for the telltale runaway locomotive sound. From the depths of the Earth, we send up fearful hopes and desperate prayers that the storm will pass us by and skip our house.

But for some houses, there is no escaping the path of destruction.

If you're reading this book, maybe your house has been hit. Maybe you are standing in the rubble of what once was and longing for a 'home' to which we have no way of returning. Those of us who have endured a big loss know what it's like to wail the siren of grief. Sometimes we let it sound. Other times we keep it silent and locked away in our throats. Still, it was us and those we love the tornado hit.

This is the story of how the sense of home was taken away from me and 'the Missing' moved into my life. My hope is you will see some of yourself in my journey, and that by giving grief a name, those of us who find ourselves feeling homeless or orphaned will drift ever closer to hope.


## RUDE AWAKENINGS

I first noticed the Missing hovering near my mother. Its dark rotation swirled above her.

Mom was curled up on one side of a bed made for two. Her poor excuse for a feather pillow was squashed over her head, a familiar sight for me. I'd often tiptoed into her room as a child in the early afternoon to interrupt her self-designated 'quiet time.'

Thinking dainty ballerina thoughts, I'd attempted to skip the steps at my sister's house that might groan under my weight and quietly made my way to peek through the crack in the guest room door where Mom lay sleeping. The Missing lay in the spot where my father should have been. It was an unfamiliar presence, or perhaps it was an absence. A gaping absence split open—leaving empty space for the Missing to enter in and bringing with it the fearful anticipation of something terrible.

I'd flown a thousand miles the night before to be there. My mom and my younger sister Lisa had been on hospital duty for weeks already, alternating shifts to be with my dad. I could hear their exhaustion through the phone at my home in Wichita, Kansas. The strain in their voices drew me north to be with them in Winnipeg, Manitoba. I wanted to ease their burden—*to join in with the burden?* Either way, I, at the very least, could be another body in the rotation of family to be in the room.

Having gotten in late at night, I hadn't been able to yet greet my mom. I missed her. Though I'd been on my own for years and was nearly three decades old, I often still needed my mommy.

Pushing the guest room door open and stepping inside, I looked forward to getting the mom hug I expected. I thought maybe we could sit and have our coffee together before we headed to the hospital to relieve my sister who was already there.

I gently rubbed my mom's back, noticing her arm wrapped tightly in surgical bandages. Instead of the sleepy, warm greeting of the reunion I anticipated, Mom's eyes barely cracked before they closed again.

"Hi, Laura, I'll be up in a bit. I need to sleep a little longer."

Slightly jilted, I tucked tail and retreated back up the creaky stairs to my air mattress on the floor. A sick pit formed in my stomach, and I realized this wasn't a normal visit. And clearly, I had no idea what I was in for.

Mom didn't intend to be cold or distant. She wasn't that at all. I was simply oblivious to how tired she was. Hours upon hours spent in the hospital had incapacitated my mama bear, sending her into deep hibernation—capable of only the most minimal basic functioning.

In some ways, I didn't recognize the head beneath the pillow.

Something was missing. Or someone. A someone who was being replaced by an unknown hovering presence; a wall of darkness was moving in. A presence that was taking up my father's side of the bed and sending my mother into an exhausted haze.

The dull, lifeless exhaustion in her eyes flickered up at me before they closed again.

The Missing had begun its rude introduction.

Later, when Mom awoke, it was all business. Oh, she hugged me. She gave me a one-armed hug only a mama can give before checking her purse to be sure she had parking money. We poured our coffee into to-go mugs. There would be no indulgent, leisurely morning cup with my mother.

Although I was a visitor who wasn't around very often, my visit was of secondary importance.

I drove while Mom navigated from the passenger's seat. She was unable to drive with her broken wrist; her face was drawn with pain. Pain in her arm, and pain in her soul. A pain that seeped and settled in her clenched jaw.

The Missing sat in the rear seat. I could feel it at my back. I was being chased even as we sat in the same car.

I didn't know what I would be walking into.

Mom's short, quick steps led me through hospital doors, past people gathering, having slow cups of coffee, and grabbing quick donuts. Canadians love their coffee and donuts.

We wove through hallways and into an elevator. I tried to take mental notes on how to get back to my parents' minivan just in case. Perhaps I was planning my own escape. By the time the elevator lurched to a stop, the pit in my stomach had grown to a cinder block. The scent of sterile hallways and urine filled my nostrils. The tornado was approaching.

The sterile hallway went on forever, flanked by doors on either side. I followed Mom into the last room on the right. In it were two beds, divided by curtains. My dad's bed was closest to the door, tucked into the shadows.

I stepped forward to greet my father, but instead I found the Missing in his place.

Dad's eyes were closed and covered by a washcloth. My father had always been larger than life, and the occupant of this hospital bed was too small to be him.

I reached forward and touched his soft shoulder.

"Hey, Dad."

I had been told he may not know who I was at first.

"It's me, Laura. I'm here."

Dad peeked out from under the washcloth and his raspy baritone voice replied,

"You're here. Lisa. My daughter."

I didn't know how much to correct him. It wasn't uncommon for him to mix our names up regularly, even in our childhood. So, I just bent down to kiss his cheek. I startled when he pulled away from me, and his raspy voice took on a frantic searching,

"Jolene?"

Mom used her one available arm to push me out of the way, grabbing a Tupperware container nearby and holding it up to Dad's mouth so he could vomit.

The smell of my shampoo had been too much for him.

Dad had been diagnosed with Renal Cell Carcinoma, or kidney cancer. The official diagnosis had come eight years prior to this. He was no stranger to the hospital. However, this time was different. The cancer had spread to his brain. At one point he'd had a tumor the size of a lime removed. Smaller tumors had also been zapped and managed by gamma knife radiation.

His most recent gamma knife procedure had been on the 4th of July. This date is secure in my memory because Dad had cheekily dropped this gem of a dad joke every time he'd gotten a chance:

"You will have fireworks going off in the sky, and I'll have fireworks going off in my brain!"

We laughed it off. Unfortunately, following this particular procedure, his brain began to bleed, and he slipped into uncontrollable seizures as his brain flooded with blood.

I sat at home in Kansas with my two-year-old son, Jude. He ate a bomb pop popsicle while I wept and prayed that God would spare my daddy.

The seizures started in the middle of the night. In the commotion of my mom helping Dad down the stairs, she slipped and fell, gashing the top of her head and breaking her wrist. By the time Lisa arrived on the scene, there was blood everywhere, and Mom and Dad were both on the floor.

I took the Tupperware from my mom and rinsed it out in the adjoining bathroom's sink.

Lisa had been there all night to keep watch over my dad who, despite his mind being unclear and his eyesight blurry, kept trying to get up and out of bed. He was afraid of the night noises and became anxious when he didn't see anyone he recognized. He wasn't accustomed to being bedridden for so long.

We sent Lisa home to shower and nap just as Dad's mother, my Grandma Stoesz, arrived with my aunt to visit.

"My son, my son. Oh God, heal my son," she tearfully prayed, stroking his head as she'd likely done when he was a child.

She was Michelangelo's *Pieta* to me. My gentle grandma and her firstborn. In his suffering, she didn't stop being his mother.

The one who cleaned scraped knees. Held his hands as he learned to walk. Fed and nurtured and guided him into adulthood.

Now my grandma's son lay helpless in a hospital bed, unable to even lift his head.

Mom walked Grandma back down to the parking lot. Before they left, Mom handed me her worn brown leather Bible and instructed me to read the Psalms for my dad,

"Hearing God's Word seems to comfort him."

I was hyper-aware of the other patient occupying the bed on the other side of the curtain. Part of me didn't want to disturb or offend him with my Bible reading, but I decided to ignore my reservations and began to read.

I started with Psalm 91. I read about the deadly pestilence and the shelter of the Most High. I read about not being afraid of the terror of the night, nor the arrow that flies by day. I choked out the words in verses 14-16:

*"Because he loves me, says the Lord, I will rescue him;… He will call on me, and I will answer him…. with long life I will satisfy him."*

The Missing reminded me that no one loved God like my father.

I'd heard my dad claim this verse over himself for the past eight years again and again. My dad and mom believed that God would grant Dad a long life. Death was not an option. It wasn't something that we discussed.

The Missing sat with me. Closely. Too closely. The room became suffocatingly small as the Missing stole my oxygen.

I continued to obediently read through the Psalms. Mom was right; Dad seemed more at peace. So, I kept reading until my voice grew hoarse. I kept reading even as the Missing mocked me.

A boiling tea kettle hissed in my ear as I read, *"Mightier than the thunder of the great waters, mightier than the breakers of the sea—The Lord on high is mighty." (Psalms 93:4)*

The Missing continued to send hot, steaming doubts and questions into the stale air.

I leaned as far as I could away from it. This presence I had never known, but it seemed to only grow in size as I contorted my body away from it, seeking distance. Space. Breathing room.

The Psalmist's proclamation of God's beautiful promises contrasted glaringly against my current reality. With each hiss, the Missing inflated in size filling the room with its presence, siphoning all the air. In that moment, when I could scarcely breathe, my dad turned his palms over and raised them to heaven.

"Yes, Lord," the baritone voice croaked out from beneath the washcloth.

Lifting his hands in worship was something my father did often. As much as getting out of bed was a reflex—so was praise.

The Missing dissipated in a rush of familiarity.

I finally recognized my father.

## ABBA'S DAUGHTER

Hours later, the doctor came in and said they were going to move my dad to another room. His nausea seemed more under control. I gathered what few belongings had accumulated around Dad's bedside, texted my mom and sister as to where they were moving him, and followed Dad's rolling bed into the room across the hall.

This room was flooded with light. At first, I was worried Dad's sensitive brain would be overstimulated, but he seemed okay.

He asked for his glasses and put them on. Then he took them back off. Blinked a couple of times and put them back on.

"I don't know if I see better with them or without them," he said.

The nurse asked if he wanted to try sitting up in a chair by the large window next to his bed. He said yes. Slowly and methodically, she helped him sit up on the edge of the bed. She slid his feet into his brown knock-off Crocs and helped him rise to his feet, pivot slowly, and lower himself into the blue, plastic upholstered chair.

I held my breath as I watched. Praying that his knees wouldn't buckle.

The Missing pointed out to me how skinny his legs looked, two knobby knees sticking out below his hospital gown.

Sitting in the chair by the window, he again asked for his glasses. I handed them to him again; he put them on and looked out the window. Then he took them off. The light streaming through the window lit up his green eyes.

The Missing disappeared in a flash of emerald. I saw my dad again.

I remembered the Robin Williams movie, "Hook," when one of the lost boys takes off Peter's glasses, smooths his wrinkles with his hands, looks into his eyes, and marvels,

*"There you are, Peter!"*

There you are, Dad. I couldn't recognize you in the shell of nausea and darkness with the Missing swarming around me and hissing in my ear.

Now much more like his typical self, he was upbeat and loud talking. He was excited that he could look out the window. I asked him if he knew whether it was day or night with the sun streaming in.

He didn't know.

I asked him what year it was.

He didn't know.

I asked him what country he lived in.

He didn't know.

I reached into my Bible and pulled out a photo I had brought of Jude and me. I tucked it into the corner of the small, broken television that sat close to Dad's bed. He squinted at the photo.

"My Jude boy!" He grabbed it and pressed it to his lips, smooching it loudly again and again. Relief smoothed the stressed-out hairs on the back of my neck. He knew me. He knew Jude.

After a while, Dad grew tired. I called the nurse to get him back to his bed and help him use the restroom. When I stepped back into the room, he was once again in the hospital bed, asleep.

Loneliness set in. My mom was on another floor of the hospital getting the stitches from her head wound taken out and having her wrist looked at. My sister was home taking a much-deserved shower and nap.

The Missing settled into the chair next to me.

For the first time since arriving, I was alone with my thoughts. I don't mind it normally, but at the time, my thoughts were hard to be with. My little family was on the cusp of something big with my husband C.J. pursuing a major career change. A change that had the potential of uprooting us and throwing me into a life that I had never anticipated for myself or my children.

I longed to talk to my father.

I wasn't sure how I felt about the whole thing, and I had hoped to get my parents' insight on the subject. They had always been there for me. They were always a phone call away. They were always ready with prayer and wisdom. *Always.*

The *always* had been replaced with the confusion of the *now.* Dad didn't even know what country he was in, and Mom was firmly stuck in exhausted trauma. Their prayer quota was being met with each agonizing moment. My own potential life upheaval would have to bow out for now.

Setting my fears and worries and what ifs in a boiling pot on the back burner, I pulled out Brennan Manning's, "The Furious Longing of God"[1] and read.

*"Abba, I belong to You"*

The prayer that Brennan Manning prayed.

*"Abba"* (inhale)

*"I belong to You"* (exhale).

Abba, the Hebrew word for Daddy, or Papa.

I had always been very much a Daddy's girl, but to sit next to his bed and watch him sleep was a new experience.

My dad wasn't good at resting. He was high-energy and was always motoring around working on one thing or another. He made lists and tinkered around. Every time he visited my home in Kansas, he would tell me, "Make me a list!" Then he would spend his visit working around my house, fixing things, and hanging things up. He liked a project and did not sit idle very long. Even when he was sitting stationary, he was constantly fidgeting. If he was made to sit too long, he would grow restless.

The Missing pointed out that the only time I had seen my dad nap was on Sunday afternoons—after being the first one to church, preaching a sermon, and then being the last to leave. Only then, with golf or tennis on the T.V. screen, would I find Dad fast asleep on the couch.

My Abba.

Watching him sleep in the hospital was different.

It was the medicine. It was the fact that he was especially anxious at night and couldn't sleep, so when the sun came up, he was exhausted.

It was a peaceful sleep, but it was also a reminder that Dad wasn't himself.

He was afraid of nighttime. Fear, just like naps, was not something I would ever have equated with my dad. He was fearless.

## ABBA'S CALLING

Dad loved telling the story of how God called him off the potato truck in rural Manitoba, Canada, and into one of the most poverty-stricken neighborhoods in the U.S.: South Central Los Angeles. There, he and Mom met through a non-profit ministry organization called World Impact. They married, and all four of us Stoesz children were born in that community.

He and Mom raised us in the inner city. They held Bible clubs and planted churches. They were passionate about bringing Jesus to the urban poor and forming healthy churches where people could tangibly experience God's love.

Despite the crime and violence, Dad loved the city. He loved the culture. He loved the people. It was not uncommon for him to pull up alongside a group of gang members, roll down his window, and ask them how their families were doing. I was taught as a young child to just *"say hi"* as we moved among the homeless or gang members. They were simply people who were a part of my childhood.

The majority of Dad's adult life was spent in South Central L.A. Later on, we took a sabbatical year in the highlands of Guatemala before moving to Wichita, Kansas. There I met my husband C.J., and my parents relocated back to Dad's hometown of Winnipeg, Manitoba to be near his folks. C.J. and I stayed in Wichita.

Dad was a fast walker and loud talker. He had an aura of self-assurance that came from a supernatural security in his identity. He was quick to point people to Jesus. He dove readily into prayer and could preach a sermon at the drop of a hat.

Watching my dad sleep after having a fearful and restless night was foreign. The Missing leaned in closely and pointed at how white was creeping through Dad's normally brown mustache. How yellow his skin looked. The faint bulge above his ear where the swelling on his brain strained against his skull.

My mom came in with her belongings and loaded them into the locker near the doorway. It was amazing what she could accomplish with one arm in a sling. Her face was gray from pain.

Mom is tough, but I could tell the pain in her wrist was getting to her. The doctor had already had to set it twice. To this day, the bone protrudes in an out-of-place way. The Missing likes to point this out every time she hands me a bowl to set on the table.

The doctor came in to explain that, now that the seizures seemed to be under control, the next focus would be to get him walking again. Bleeding on the brain has the possibility of being reabsorbed by the body. As the bleeding subsides, mental functions return.

The doctor had to spell this out to me a couple of times.

*So we could get Dad back?*

*Hope*

They would be sending a physical therapy specialist down to work with Dad to get him onto his feet and walking with a walker. He would also have to climb three stairs to practice getting in his own front door at home.

*Home*

Once again, I found myself alone with my sleeping Dad.

The physical therapist came in. She looked to be about the same age as me. Dad could have easily been her dad too.

I shook his shoulder, "Dad, you need to wake up. The physical therapist is here to work with you."

His eyes didn't open. I bent closer to his ear,

"Dad, it's time to practice walking," I said loudly.

Still nothing.

I grabbed a wet washcloth and applied it to his forehead, a trick that I would use with infant Jude when I needed him to wake up to eat.

"WAKE UP, DAD!" I nearly shouted.

Nothing. He simply snored on.

Helplessly I looked at the physical therapist and apologized. I couldn't wake him. The Missing wrapped its hand around my throat,

"Can you come back later?" I choked out.

Her own teary eyes met mine, and she nodded.

The Missing stood next to me and reminded me that if Dad didn't learn to walk again, he would never leave this place. The Missing, although with me, had a way of filling the room with loneliness instead of presence.

*Abba, I belong to You.*

*Abba, I belong to You.*

In and out I breathed. I breathed in the sickening smell of the hospital: bleach and bodily fluids. The Missing waved the smell of my parent's home under my nose: food and laundry on the line. With the stark contrast, the Missing rotated the cinder block in my gut. It landed heavy and hard.

I tried to pray away the dense loneliness punctuated by the smell of antiseptic. The absence of the familiar. The silence, void of audible reassurance.

I longed for the Dad that had been. Although he lay sleeping within arm's reach, I missed the safety of his presence. The fullness of the Dad I knew and loved.

The Missing settled in and began to recite the *"what ifs."* It began to introduce the unthinkable. To casually mention the unmentionable.

*Abba, I belong to You.*

*Abba, I belong to You.*

Reader, I tell this story with as much vivid detail as I can recall, to draw you into the place where the Missing moved in. Perhaps in your own life, you can recall the time you began to notice the dark clouds circling over your head. Maybe in looking back into your story, you can identify when the Missing was approaching or beginning to make its vacant presence known.

Perhaps in your specific loss, there was no warning—it was a violent storm that formed out of the blue to flip your life upside down in one fell swoop.

However it happened, whether it was a gradual arrival or with no warning, the Missing moved in.

---

*It sat on my chest; its bony knees pushed against my throat. Somehow it was both agile and heavy. I struck at it, but my fists failed to make any kind of contact. I realized as my arms flailed in frenzied, futile panic that the Missing was more nebulous than solid. It was oozing and oppressive. It easily overtook me.*

*Its nails were filed into sharp points and left five red crescent-shaped marks on each of my wrists. They stung in a high-pitched tone that hung in the air. I could feel the pain in my ears—a mosquito's persistent hum. With each shallow inhale, I breathed in the wretched smell of sterile hospital hallways and wilted lilies.*

## CHAPTER 2

# The Missing's Approach

Something grief will teach you quickly is how little you know. Everything you thought was certain suddenly becomes uncertain. It's completely disorienting.

I never pictured a life without my dad. He was a fixture in my past and when I envisioned my future, he was there. His presence, I thought, was a given. His voice, his ability to provide guidance, his opinions and know-how—all of this, I thought, would be knitted into the fabric of what is the rest of my life.

There comes a point where you begin to realize how tattered and holey this tapestry of life is becoming. The Missing takes over. It sits at its loom and begins to weave a new life; one you hardly recognize.

Dad eventually climbed the three steps up to his red front door and into his new normal.

We nearly lost him again in August 2012 to another round of uncontrollable seizures. The doctors were able to stabilize him, but he would never be the same again.

Talking became even more of a struggle for him. He mixed up words and spoke slowly. Slurring. Stuttering. Gone was his brisk, intentional walk. Now he took slow, shuffle steps with a walker when he wasn't in his leather chair by the window.

That being said, he never forgot our Thursday phone call. Every Thursday, as he had done for a couple of years before, he would call me. We'd started this habit in an effort to keep connected across the distance and within the busyness of both of our schedules. My name was written in his planner for every Thursday.

At my home in Wichita, it was easy for me to remove myself from the pain of the Missing. The Missing's main camp was in Canada. It would mainly visit me on Thursdays in the middle of broken syllables and slurred pronunciation of simple words.

My mom, sister, and brother-in-law were the ones for whom there was no escape from the Missing. They were there for every doctor's appointment. They counted pills and clung to hope. I was well aware they withheld some information from me in their regular phone call updates, attempting to shield me from some of the deeper traumas. The gaps in between were easily filled by the Missing. Fear seeped into every nook and cranny of the unknowns.

## ANTICIPATION

I was in a fragile state. Along with Dad's cancer battle, C.J. was in the process of joining the military. It was a mere signature on some paperwork and a sworn oath to a flag that stood between me and complete life upheaval. My older brother, Aaron, had entered into his own season of loss and was now living with us.

I had also learned I was expecting my second child.

I fought first-trimester nausea and clung to Jude's pudgy hand as his daddy swore to serve and protect his country. It all felt so surreal—as though a movie version of my life was playing out before my eyes.

As my tall, strong husband and best friend executed his very first clumsy salute, the actress that looked like me smiled—even managed to have a tearful look of pride in her eyes. *That couldn't be me, surely.* As the descendant of staunch pacifists, I wasn't even sure if I believed in war. Yet here I was, standing by smiling, agreeing to let C.J. sign our life away.

These enormous changes warranted enormous discussions with the people I felt safest with. With the people I'd gone to for counsel my entire life. But I'd been cut off. My Thursday phone calls with Dad had been stripped to the bare bones—me praying, while Dad cried silent tears on the other end. Words became lodged in his brain, spinning around in confused delirium until they fizzled into nonsense syllables I was left to make sense of.

My pastor for life—silenced.

This was the man whose voice was more familiar to me than even my own. I had studied it for years sitting in his congregation. I knew the frequency at which it would crack. I could predict the swallow of water he would inevitably take about three-quarters of the way through his sermon. I knew when the spit would start flying and the tears would begin to soften the volume in shaky emotion.

Some people might find poetry in a pastor who could no longer talk.

I found it horrific and traumatic

The Missing replayed, again and again, the sound of that baritone voice, calling up the stairs for me to come down for dinner. The inflections and pitch lodged themselves securely in my mind.

Now, the sound of clear words—his wisdom—was gone. They were now missing and absorbed into the before.

Mute.

There came some Thursdays that I couldn't bring myself to answer the phone.

I keep my old phone that contains the voicemails from those days. They are the slow, methodical messages of an imitation voice. A voice trying to be something it once was. A shadow of the familiar. A voice telling me in broken syllables it loves me and worries that I am going too hard. To "tell Jude-boy I love him."

All at once the whole person and a figment.

I've since learned what I was experiencing was "anticipatory grief." This is full grief in and of itself. Those who have lost a loved one to illness or age see the Missing coming. It begins to affect their life before the passing away even happens. Their loved one declines slowly. Piece by piece, the losses happen.

The Missing yanked me by the arm into the darkness of grief. Grief I wasn't sure I was allowed to feel yet because Dad wasn't quite gone. He was fading, but still there. And he and Mom communicated again and again that they believed God was going to heal him. There was no room for doubt. Their message to me was clear: We must cling to absolute faith. We must not doubt because then Dad would die.

I fell apart in my book club which wasn't actually a book club because we did very little reading. We mostly drank wine and talked about real life.

I caught a glimpse of myself already shrouded in the Missing's presence—a figment in my own right—reflected back through the eyes of my dear friends. Their mouths hung open in helpless shock while one of them gently told me she thought I could, "benefit from some counseling."

*Was this really my life?*

Have you ever looked around at your life and didn't recognize it? Everything seems to be out of focus. It's hard to make sense of what you're looking at. What once was a wonderful, easy, and beautiful life begins to morph into something you don't want it to. Sometimes it's our own choices that put us there, but oftentimes in life, I'm finding there are things outside of our control that just—happen. And we are left struggling to make sense of the nonsensical.

At night, I begged God to have mercy on me. I was surrounded by pain, my back broken into unending limbo.

When I delivered the news to C.J. about another baby being on the way, he'd responded, "Do we have to talk about this now?"

His emotions were worn threadbare in this season too. The intensity of the military calling he felt and all that lay before him was overwhelming enough as it was. Adding another child on top of everything else— I laughed and rolled my eyes, but it stung. I tempered my celebration. We had wanted this child, but with pain and uncertainty closing in on every side, I begged God to protect my baby from second-hand stress from the fear the Missing poured over my head. Fear seeped into every pore, covering me in cold dread.

It was coming, and I knew it. I was a Kansas girl trying to keep my balance in the gusting winds, and with the scent of tornadoes already in the air, all I could do was helplessly watch and wait for the approaching storm.

*Abba, I belong to You.*


## THE COLD OF CHRISTMAS

A couple of months later, Jude and I flew up to Winnipeg on our own. C.J. and my brother Aaron were going to drive up and join us there later for Christmas.

Driving from the airport, Jude saw the piles of snow the plows pushed into enormous mounds and exclaimed, "Mountains!" Typical Kansan.

Winnipeg at Christmastime is cold. Not just chilly, nor that magical kind of cold given its twinkle by the delicious contrast of 'cozy.' It is the type of cold that hurts. It's the deep ache that begins to throb when the temperature-induced Novocain takes effect and requires many itchy woolen layers and copious amounts of coffee and tea in an effort to thaw out your insides.

The numb feeling invading my toes took me back to the many times Dad had laced up my ice skates as a kid. I was a terrible ice skater. I was afraid of falling, or worse, falling through the ice. Irrationally so. Even at manmade ice rinks with only an inch worth of ice, I couldn't help but picture myself trapped in the frigid water underneath and, unable to find the hole where the ice had broken, reduced to wide eyes and bubbles where screams should be.

Still, Dad was determined every time our California-born selves would come to visit the great white North, we would tap into the maple syrup roots that run deep on our Canadian sides. We would skate and sled—and we would like it.

I'm afraid I'm still guilty of having a romanticized version of snow in my head, though, in my experience, it inevitably turns into a *'million needles stabbing every exposed appendage'* experience.

Like that time it snowed once in the five years we lived here in Georgia—a monumental half an inch that was gone by mid-morning. The kids screamed and scrambled for jackets. I couldn't find gloves or mittens, so I put socks on their hands and waterproofed them with tape.

For about ten minutes, everything was magical. Then reality hit. The needles quickly made their way through the socks and tape to their warm southern fingers and began their sharp immunization against any fluffy, romantic notions I may have had.

Whiny requests for hot cocoa quickly commenced.

How often it is that our expectations do not line up with reality. Dashed expectations are a frustrating and even humbling experience. Amid anticipatory grief, one learns quickly not to have expectations. You are at the mercy of a failing human body.

I had been so looking forward to spending Christmas with Mom and Dad. It had been years since we had been to Winnipeg for the holiday and having them host us would be somewhat like it was when we were kids.

Or so I thought.

Seeing Dad this time was the same sharp, needling reminder of the painful cold which chokes out the magic of snow.

The Missing owned the room.

Dad's mustache was now completely white, as though frostbite had succeeded in taking over his upper lip. The whites of his eyes were yellow, and the green of them—lopsided. They gazed around or beside what he was trying to look at. His smile sloped.

Any romantic notions of *"coming home for Christmas"* were blown into oblivion by the Missing's rush of frigid air.

This Christmas would be nothing like when we were kids. Nothing like what I was hoping for.

I found myself frantically searching for the familiar. *Was there anything untouched and untainted by the Missing?*

There comes a time when everything you see or experience is colored by the pallor of grief, even things that should be familiar and comforting. Gradually they too are tinged by sadness and the unknown.

Many of my parents' ornaments and decorations were the same. Built by my father, the wooden stable with its porcelain figurines sat in its place atop the piano. It remained unchanged. Well, except for the virgin Mary and baby Jesus, whom Mom had decided were too Aryan looking. They had been replaced with darker, more realistic counterparts. The camels we'd decorated as kids stood by, as well as the owl that I had painted into a ghastly looking brown thing, until Dad redeemed it with the most delicate painted feathers on its chest.

The smell of Christmas tea and peppernuts hung in the air. Peppernuts or *Pfeffernusse* are tiny gingerbread-like cookies that you eat by the handful. They are a staple in Mennonite households at Christmas. The Missing's constant, hovering presence drove me to eat handful after handful of them until my stomach hurt. Stress eating runs in the family, although the Missing had stolen that too.

A well-meaning someone had casually mentioned to Dad that "sugar feeds cancer." My ever-fearless father, from whom I'd inherited my insatiable sweet tooth, was now afraid to even eat one cookie for fear it would *"feed the cancer"* and be his demise.

People can be so careless in what they say. Those of us who grieve know this well. We bear the scars of trite platitudes and unsolicited advice.

Instead of anything especially delicious, Mom had made a pot of pumpkin soup. Not one to ever waste food, they had been eating its leftovers for more than a week. Dad's eyes told me how tired he was of the soup, but he ate it to please Mom—and, perhaps, to continue to feed the hope they both held that maybe, if he ate healthy enough, the cancer would disappear.

This year, the Missing also robbed Dad of his traditional tree duties.

Every year growing up, we would get a real tree, and every year Dad would battle it into its tree stand. The only time I ever heard my dad cuss was when it was Dad versus tree. He rarely got angry, but a crooked Christmas tree was enough to send steam out of his ears and PG expletives out of his mouth.

One year, he hurled the tree stand into the garbage can and jammed the bottom of the tree into a 10-gallon bucket full of sand. He then tied a string around the trunk and nailed it to the wall to keep it straight.

Now, the much smaller, non-artificial tree that had been arranged in the corner behind Dad's chair was a clear sign his tree-wrestling days were in the past. Although he could still perform small tasks, the majority of the decorating had been accomplished by Mom.

Dad was sensitive to light and sound and needed frequent naps. I did my best to keep my boisterous toddler calm and happy, but when Jude got worked up or whiny, I noticed Dad struggled more with managing simple things.

The Missing leaned heavily on my shoulders at sundown while I watched Dad struggle to close the front window blinds. His fingers fiddled with the cord. When it became clear to me that Dad was stumped, I gently took the small pulley from his hands and closed them.

Tearfully, Dad shuffled back to his chair. The Missing, the bully that it is, had put him back in his place.

## GATHERING

Dad's side of the family loves their family gatherings—Christmas being one of the main occasions for us all to get together. Living as far away as I do, it was a rare and wonderful treat to be able to join them with C.J. and Jude.

The Stoesz clan consists of my grandpa and grandma, their five kids (Dad being the oldest), and all their kids and grandkids. Dad, normally extroverted and fully invested in visiting with his family, sat in the front room away from the action to avoid getting overstimulated.

The looks in my relatives' eyes were that of concern. Their own pain was reflected there as they sought to maintain a respectful distance. They had no choice but to take their cue from Mom, who, in her own typical stubbornness, was dogmatically choosing to believe that Dad would be healed.

I have yet to decide whether this is one of the greatest examples of faith I've ever witnessed or a manner of coping that put us firmly into a state of collective denial. Yet, everyone but my mother was thinking it—

*This was probably Dad's last Christmas gathering.*

When I was younger, we once accidentally locked our cat, Velvet, in the upstairs closet as we were leaving on vacation. By the time we came home, ten days later, she was a malnourished, dehydrated, skeleton of a black cat.

We all cried big tears while she meowed her relief.

Years later, she again mistakenly got out of the house. Mom and Dad drove up and down the neighborhood, finally finding her being chased by a flock of crows determined that she was to be their dinner.

Like Velvet, Dad was a cat with nine lives, though nobody was quite sure which life he was on. He loved to tell the story of when he was a newborn baby and the doctors couldn't understand why baby Fred wasn't gaining weight. They ran out of options and sent Grandma and Grandpa home with their infant son, fully expecting him to die.

Grandma and Grandpa decided they would dedicate this child to God's service should he live. They went to one last doctor who discovered a blockage in the tiny baby's intestines. He operated, and Dad lived. A pearly four-inch scar on Dad's round belly told the story.

In his sermons, he loved to preach about *'purpose.'*

"God has a plan for you! Just as He has a plan for me."

I struggle often with what my purpose is. Christians especially seem determined to wrench *'purpose'* out of their life, as if that makes us more worthy of God's love. Maybe we all have the same broad purpose that fleshes out in a trillion ways, and it's up to us to decide how to spend this one life we are given. Maybe being loved by the one in whose image we were created is enough. Maybe if we can fully grasp this, the rest will follow.

At his initial diagnosis in 2004, the doctors gave Dad six months to a year to live. Eight years later, the doctors had again given him a prognosis of weeks. Four months on, we were surrounded by relatives at the Christmas family gathering.

There was one thing of which we were all certain, he was already a walking miracle.

Despite this, the weariness showed in my sister Lisa's eyes as she smiled her way through the family gathering. She has a way of smiling with her whole face, eyes disappearing into squinty lines. The youngest of the four of us and a nurse by profession, she had endured a front-row seat for the past eight years. She was Mom's shoulder to lean on and the official translator for all medical jargon.

They could communicate from across the room with a quick nod or facial expression. Lisa could read Mom's thoughts and immediately step into action, gathering belongings or finding scarves, jackets, and shoes.

Aaron and I, on the other hand, were the outsiders. Though we were the older siblings, our little sister had become the leader of the family. Any authority we'd had at one time felt because of our birth order had been deferred.

Jude was a delightful distraction. Comfortable in a room full of strangers, he was engaging and animated, wooing the world with his sweet and positive personality. He was (and still is) very much his grandpa's grandson.

We used him, and his bedtime as a thinly veiled exit excuse. Everyone knew that it was actually Dad that needed to head home. Away from the excitement, festive noises, sights, and smells that overwhelmed his senses.

Back to his chair by the window.

It's a strange topsy turvy alternate reality to become a caregiver to someone who once cared for you. You walk a tightrope strung high above a windy canyon, balancing between preserving their individual autonomy and making decisions for them before they reach their ever-changing limits. More than anything you want them to be capable of doing what they once did and be who they once were. More than anything you want the Missing to leave and for all to be restored as it should be.

But it's really hard to stay atop a tightrope, especially in a tornado.

## FOOTPRINTS AND STITCHES

The next day, I sat in Dad's chair and watched out the front window as he and Jude played in the snow. Dad shuffled along, not lifting his feet as he walked, leaving tracks of parallel lines instead of footprints.

The Missing replayed a time we'd walked to my grandpa's church in the snow when I was a child. I didn't want to get my feet wet wearing only thin tights in my shiny church shoes.

"Just walk in my footprints," Dad had advised.

Frozen in my memory is the image of my little girl foot stepping gingerly into dad-sized, snowy, yet solid footprints, keeping my white tights dry.

Now he was mindful of every step—cautious not to fall on his unsteady, unreliable legs and artificial hips. I watched him pick up snow and form it with his mittened hands into a ball, showing Jude. The trauma to his brain had managed to age him into an ancient old man, while simultaneously reducing him to an almost adorable state of childlikeness.

He held the snowball to his mustached face and took a bite of the clean, powdery snow. Jude followed suit, forming snowballs and eating them. Mom scurried along after them, a mother hen and her chicks, chasing them with her camera.

When I was seven, my parents led a church excursion to the mountains in California to find snow. Elated at the adventure and banking on my Canadian roots for an inherent knowledge of how to steer, I excitedly grabbed a toboggan and pointed it downhill. On my first run down the hill, I ran into a tree stump, slicing a large gash in my chin.

When my mom reached me, I was unconscious and gushing blood.

Dad rushed me to the nearest emergency room where we had to wait hours for them to give me 14 stitches in my chin and determine that my right heel was fractured. It easily became the most eventful day of my young life. I remember being relieved and a little in awe that it was Dad who took me to the ER. I also felt a little guilty.

To end up spending the entire day in the ER was not in Dad's plan. The ministry often took top priority in our family life and the people that had come to the mountains with us were important to him. Nevertheless, he was there with me. And, as he held my head still and gripped my hand tightly and the doctor stuck large needles into my chin to numb the pain—I felt the comfort of his presence. I squeezed my eyes shut. His presence made me brave. His reassurance was the courage I needed to hold still and let the stitching happen.

Now, it was my turn to be there for him. And so, since Dad was unable to take Jude sledding himself this time—we did it for him. None of us really wanted to trudge up the steep nearby sled hill and battle the sharp needles in our toes. But we did it anyway for the man whose footprints we'd walked in our entire lives. We knew it would make him happy. It was a part of his legacy we could already begin to live out.

Maybe even now, as he sat sidelined in his brown chair by the window observing rather than participating, it helped a little knowing we would continue to break snowy paths in his honor. The tradition of snowy fun would live on for generations to come.

## GIFTS AND GOODBYES

Mom and Dad were never big on gifts. It was partially because they had taken a vow of poverty when entering full-time ministry and joining World Impact, so financially it wasn't always possible. But there also wasn't a materialistic bone in either of their bodies. Neither of them came from wealth. Mom was the daughter of a Kansas farmer; Dad was the son of a small, country school headmaster and pastor.

One Christmas long ago, my siblings and I begged and begged for a Nintendo game system. Many of our friends had them, and we felt as if we were the only kids on the planet without.

Traditionally, my parents allowed us to open one present on Christmas Eve. On this particular Christmas, there was a large rectangular box addressed to the four of us that we were *sure* was a Nintendo.

My mom cringed in the corner as we excitedly tore into the wrapping paper. Oldest brother Aaron led the frenzied charge and was quickly diffused when we opened the box only to find four pairs of sweatpants neatly folded amongst the tissue paper.

Mom was horrified, and Dad was amused as they sent our disappointed and humbled selves to bed.

Rather than gifting us material possessions, they were much more likely to give us experiences that would build memories. Their gift this Christmas for C.J. and me was dinner out at a quaint French restaurant on the mighty Red River. Auntie Lisa gleefully babysat Jude, and C.J and I went out with Mom and Dad for a delicious meal.

Dad ordered the French onion soup and declined dessert.

After dinner, we went for a quick walk in the winter air. The streetlamps bounced off the white snow, sparkling like diamonds. I linked arms with Dad, and he shuffled along. I don't know which of us was holding the other up—him with his failing body and me with my center of gravity bloating woefully with baby and dinner.

I can still feel his arm in mine. The crook of it soft. Secure yet unsteady. Arm in arm, my dad and me. The Missing was in the cold that penetrated through my boots to my toes.

Needles.

The next day we said goodbye.

I knew.

Without really knowing, I knew.

This would be the last time I saw Dad in person on this side of eternity.

He sat in his chair by the window.

I found myself instinctively crawling entirely into his lap as I had done so often as a child. This time, I awkwardly folded over my just-starting-to-show pregnant belly. I wrapped my arms around his shoulders and leaned my face into his neck.

I was once again the fearful 7-year-old in the emergency room, clinging tightly to my daddy while the needles approached my flesh.

This time rather than a stitching, it was a tearing.

The Missing floated up my nostrils in an awareness that Dad already smelled different.

Gone was his typical scent of motor oil and soap. Instead, I smelled aging, medicine, and pumpkin soup.

He and I wept.

We wept because there were no words. They were stuck in choked-up throats and a damaged brain.

There was only the desperate clinging that happens when letting go feels wrong and impossible. There was only the knowing without really knowing.

There was only the Missing.

---

*Helplessly, I watched it move in with its imposing black suitcase full of "should have beens." Those, it unpacked and displayed around my home. Framed with mocking intentions, my unmet expectations and dead dreams were now everywhere I looked.*

*It dragged its fingers along everything I called mine, leaving oily prints. Nothing was left untouched.*

*The slightest brush of its finger against my skin left a bruise. Soon, every inch of me was painful purple, battered by its mere presence. It made a point to push on my bruises without letting up so that the pain hovered—*

*Persistent. Constant. Aching.*

## CHAPTER 3

# The Missing Moves In

The month before the large brain bleed that would signal the beginning of the end for Dad, I found myself standing in line with him for a huge roller coaster called "Goliath." We'd met as a family in California to take a trip down memory lane and decided to visit our favorite theme park.

The protective daughter in me was all too aware of the cancer that had been slowly invading his body for the past eight years. My eyes nervously skimmed the warning signs posted along the line's route, clearly stating who should not ride the thrill ride.

Referencing the sign, I encouraged my dad to duck out of line and head back to my mom to wait for us. He waved me off with a shake of his head.

Growing more concerned as the line moved forward, I continued to broach the subject. Finally growing exasperated, he cut me off with a sharp,

"Laura! I can't be afraid to live!"

And that was that. And we survived the ride to tell the story.

He wasn't afraid. In fact, I never saw him afraid until the cancer in his brain tricked him into it.

I often wonder what it would be like to be fearless. To willingly take a seat at the very front of a roller coaster. To release my hands from the safety harness and let gravity happen. I'm a middle-car kind of gal. I protect my neck and cover my rear.

I am not fearless. In fact, I have battled fear my entire life. The roller coaster we found ourselves on with my dad's cancer journey was no exception. C.S. Lewis' quote from his precious little book *A Grief Observed* rings ever true,

*"No one ever told me that grief felt so like fear."* [2]

They are close comrades—Grief and Fear. They feel very much the same.

Dad was initially incorrectly diagnosed with bone cancer. Later, they determined it had actually originated in the kidney. The symptom that drove him to finally seek medical help was a sore hip.

At my wedding in May 2004, Dad walked with a limp, my arm linked in his, side by side down the aisle to my young groom.

I found out via phone call while on my honeymoon that the doctor suspected cancer.

The fear that the mere mention of cancer pushes into your life is intense. No, cancer is not a death sentence. Modern medicine has come a long way in treating it. All of us know of someone who has had it and emerged cancer free. Modern medicine and the grace of God kept Dad alive for nine years past his cancer diagnosis. His doctors were amazed that he lived as long as he did. At the time of his death, he was the longest living kidney cancer survivor in Manitoba.

The cancer was Goliath, and for the majority of the journey, Dad was an unafraid David. Coming at it with sticks and stones and enormous faith.

I was able to leave the Missing largely in Canada once we returned home after Christmas. Back to our life and the uncertainty of what lay ahead of us as a military family.

Dad had a CT scan the day I found out I was having a girl. When the ultrasound tech gave me the news, my world turned pink and purple. I called my mom with the grand reveal just as Dad was getting wheeled back,

"I have a granddaughter!" he stammered to the nurses surrounding him.

A week or so later, on our Thursday phone call, I told him the name we were planning for his first grand girl—Lyla Rae. She would share my mom's middle name.

Through tears, Dad managed to tell me he loved it,

"Mom needs this."

Mom was discouraged. These were the darkest days. I could hear the strain in her voice. She found herself drawn to books about suffering. She consumed story after story about the Holocaust. She dove into personal testimonies of war and genocide and death and sorrow. I encouraged her to read some lighter material. Maybe a sappy novel, something not so depressing.

"I just can't right now, Laura." Her voice was weak through the phone.

I think taking in stories of other people's suffering helped her not feel so alone in her own pain. To see that there is survival beyond despair. To find a twisted sort of solace that her suffering was less than what others had been through. To this day she looks on those darkest days with regret. She laments that she wasn't more patient with Dad.

She doesn't give herself enough credit.

Perhaps in reading this book, you too can find solace in my journey that might somewhat mirror your own. I am under no illusions that my story is special. Yes, I will always believe my father was extraordinary, but in so many ways the loss of him feels unbelievably and frustratingly ordinary in the scope of the world.

Empathy is powerful. So are stories of perseverance and healing. I tend to be drawn more toward comedic shows with clever writing and larger-than-life characters. But it's the books and movies and shows about loss and fear and *real life* that have shaped my soul.

Laughter or lightheartedness can make us feel like we are mocking our current circumstances. Watching and reading material that evokes that response within us can be a much-needed escape. Sometimes numbness is a healthy response. We couldn't survive without emotional escape.

Other times we feel this insatiable urge to push on the bruise, and dive headfirst into another's pain or fear so we don't have to feel the anguish of the solitary. It's the validation that whatever we are feeling or have felt along the way is—normal. All we want is normal.

But nothing was normal anymore.

The Missing had taken over my parent's house. The music my mom once played now hurt my dad's head. The front curtains stayed drawn to block out light.

"Deeper into grace," Mom would say to me.

We were able to meet as an entire family on a video call. My brothers and sister and spouses. I held Jude on my lap.

Someone, I don't remember who, made the off-handed comment, "One day at a time." This prompted Dad, who could barely string two words together in a spoken sentence, to launch into singing the old hymn with perfect clarity:

*One day at a time, sweet Jesus*
*That's all I'm asking from You*
*Just give me the strength to do every day*
*What I have to do*
*Yesterday's gone, sweet Jesus*
*And tomorrow may never be mine*

*Lord, help me today, show me the way*
*One day at a time*

On a pixelated screen, glitchy with internet hiccups.
That would be the last time I would see my dad alive.

## IMMINENT

It was supposed to be a refreshing family getaway. C.J. and I were in Kansas City for some fun and relaxation. Instead, I awoke to my phone full of missed calls and voicemails from my mom and sister.

That night, Dad had stood up to use the restroom and his femur snapped. They rushed him to the hospital. They sent him in for emergency surgery to repair his femur.

I prayed a coward's prayer.

*"If you're not going to heal him all the way, just take him!"*

I wanted to get off the roller coaster.

I cried out to the unseen. I cried out to the God I had accepted into my heart as a 5-year-old child beneath a California palm tree. To the God to whom I had done my best to be obedient. I had lived each of my 30 years to the best of my ability in surrender to Him. I'd been good. I'd done right.

*He owed me!*

The problem was I knew too much. I knew He owed me nothing. I had been taught from the youngest age that God works through suffering—that suffering is promised in this life, and obedience doesn't exempt you from pain. I'd read the Psalmist's laments.

In fact, the spiteful side of my spirit was angry because this was just like something God *would* do.

Dad never came out of the anesthesia.

Further testing showed that he had multiple tumors in his spine and brain. There was nothing more that could be done. He had been in more pain than he was even able to communicate.

Mom wept when she told me they were going to make him as comfortable as possible. She cried and told me she was sorry. That she had tried.

The Missing opened its enormous jaws and swallowed me whole.

---

I stared out the dark passenger side window on the long drive home from Kansas City. C.J. reached across and held my hands. His large right hand can hold both of mine if we position them just right. We'd figured this out during our dating days. Then, it was a fun little trick; now it was my lifeline. My anchor to keep me from being swept away.

He tried to choose soothing music to play on the car stereo, but every love song that played was for my parents. For their lost love. For the broken in half. For the dreams that would never be. Every beautiful note and lovely lyric was for them.

The stars glistened softly in their places in the sky. Hovering there. Unmoving—even as the car sped and the prairie grasses rushed by. Their twinkling lights grew into blurry orbs through tears. They were frustratingly stationary when my world wouldn't stop spinning.

The Missing sprinted alongside—Its long legs easily keeping pace.

I wept.

*Abba, I belong to You.*

## FLIGHT AND FREEDOM

I flew to Winnipeg a couple of days later, not knowing if I would arrive before Dad's passing.

Again the groans of my spirit prayed a coward's prayer. Deep down where only God had a view, I hoped he would pass before I got there. I didn't want to watch Dad die.

Anticipating the moment of the last breath is a special kind of purgatory. Those who have lost someone suddenly did not have the waiting. Perhaps they would consider it a luxury to have the waiting. The limbo of time when you know the end is imminent, but the timing is still painfully ambiguous. I don't know what is worse, a slow death or a sudden one. They are both horrific. All I know is I didn't want to see it happen for my dad.

You see, he wasn't waking up anymore. There would be no profound last words. There was no unfinished business between us. No peace that needed to be made. No apologies necessary or bedside confessions.

Nothing was open-ended between us—*except everything.* It was now just the open-ended stretch of years before me that I couldn't envision without him. The gaping Missing.

I didn't want to see it happen. I didn't want to be there for his final breath. For the stillness to fall.

I was too weak. Too afraid.

He exhaled for the last time as my plane descended into the Canadian prairies.

I humor myself by thinking we passed each other in midair. *Did he pause outside my plane? Did his spirit give me a thumbs up outside the tiny oval window?*

I like to think he did it on purpose. That he intentionally spared me having to watch him labor for his last breath. He was unselfish like that and knew me well. It was a mercy he could yet give.

What was that moment like for him? The trading of this world for the next.

Was it like the scene Brennan Manning described in the book I read at Dad's bedside not so long ago, when a leprous woman on her deathbed heard these words from her Abba, drawing her into His presence?

> *Come now, my love, My lovely one, come.*
> *For you, the Winter has passed,*
> *The snows are over and gone,*
> *The flowers appear in the land,*
> *The season of Joyful songs has come.*[3]

Reading this at Dad's bedside nine months before had been my undoing. I trapped the sobs in the back of my throat and refused to give them sound. I kept the tears in the back of my eye sockets, denying them gravity down my cheeks and onto the blue vinyl upholstered chair which was my post beside Dad's hospital bed.

*Had Dad's death been like that too?* A gentle beckoning into the afterlife with a quoting of sacred text, a love letter to the good and faithful?

Or was it more like that scene in *Braveheart* with a cry of *"Freedom!!"* As my daddy's soul grew too large for the confines of his broken, human body, Jesus' hands finally came within reach, and Dad was able to grab hold of scarred palms and swing forward into Heaven's light on a trapeze of glory.

Either way, the contrast between his deathbed and the arms of Jesus must have been staggering.

For the record, I don't believe there are no tears in Heaven anymore.

Not since Dad got there anyway. I can't envision him responding in any other way to the glory of Heaven other than face down on golden asphalt.

Weeping.

While we wept here on Earth, he must have too.

## DREADFUL STEPS

Lisa met me at the airport. As soon as I saw her face, I knew. She didn't even have to say the words. He was gone. It was finished.

Or perhaps, it was just beginning.

God help me, but when I saw my sister's face, I felt relief. It was over. Or so I thought. I really had no idea what I was in for.

The Missing gripped me in its talons. I clutched my sister's hand in the back seat of my aunt and uncle's car. They drove us to the hospital. We stepped into the same familiar elevator. Like Pavlov's dog, the scent and sounds sent my breathing into a hyperventilating prayer—

*Abba, I belong to You.*

We were headed to the room where his body lay. He'd been gone less than two hours. The Missing began whirling; panic settled in, heavy and frenzied.

"I don't want to go in there." I broke down to my sister.

To my *sister* of all people.

My baby sister, who had spent the entire night before fitfully trying to sleep on two chairs pushed together at Dad's bedside with her fingers on his pulse waiting for it to stop beating. My sister, who'd taken the driver's license from the man who'd taught her how to drive after his seizure. My sister, who'd checked countless charts and counted mountains of pills. Who'd been there for the darkest days.

To my brave sister, who'd had no escape from the Missing, I expressed my cowardly panic.

"*Weakling,*" the Missing snarled down my neck.

I didn't want to see his body.

My sister didn't let go of my hand until our mom greeted us at the elevator. She grabbed me and hugged me. Tears streamed down her face and onto her smiling lips.

"Laura, come see him. He's with Jesus. He is just fine."

She pulled me into a large room, I was surprised to see it was occupied by three other beds with patients in them—witnesses to the taking. My dad's bed was in the back left corner. Mom pulled me behind the curtain and there he was.

Yellow. Mouth open.

"Feel his hands," Mom said.

The deranged, even manic look in her eyes, plus her grip on my arm and hand, were the only things keeping me from fleeing to the exit.

I reached out and brushed my fingertips against his left hand.

It was still warm.

The Missing roared in my ears, drowning out my Abba prayer.

*Get me out of here. Get me out of here. Get me out of here.*

## PREPARATIONS AND THE FIRSTBORN

The next few days are a blur.

Aaron arrived soon after I did. He pulled Dad's wool woven jacket off of the coat rack in the front entrance behind their red front door and put it on. He wore it steadily for the next few days. Wrapped in the Missing. My big brother—Dad's look-alike—was no stranger to loss. Now sullen and quiet, he was very unlike his usual talkative and fiery self.

The funeral director was affectionately nicknamed Clarence after the angel in the classic Christmas film, "It's a Wonderful Life." He had a jovial nature, white hair, and a white mustache. Much like the movie character.

He saw my round belly and quietly reflected,

"One leaves us, and another one comes."

He knew Dad. Everyone knew Dad. So we didn't have to explain to Clarence that an ornate casket would not be appropriate, nor a large flower arrangement. In his gentle shepherding manner, he initially pointed us at a basic unfinished pine box with rope handles. It looked like something pirates would be buried at sea in.

I agreed readily because I didn't want to engage any more than I absolutely had to with anything that concerned my dad's body. I didn't want to think about it. I didn't want to see it. I didn't want to imagine it being buried.

Aaron broke his stoic silence and spoke up,

"No. That one's not nice enough."

He was right. It was too simple. We opted for the slightly nicer model with the smoothly carved pine handles. Unfinished—like Dad.

Clarence talked us through options for the cemetery plots nearby. I nodded robotically. I didn't care. I just wanted the conversation over with.

Again, Aaron spoke up. The new patriarch of the family.

"No. He should be buried in Niverville. Where he was born. Where Grandma and Grandpa already have plots."

He was right again. Quiet, with his hands jammed deep into Dad's woolen pockets. He spoke, and we listened. My big brother—the firstborn of the firstborn.

The birthright of a wool jacket. In that moment, holy oil poured off his head and pooled at his feet.


## LILIES AND FORMALDEHYDE

We went back to the funeral home a few days later for the viewing. C.J. and Jude had arrived. The Missing sat on my chest, and I gasped for shallow panicked breaths. I didn't want to go in there. I didn't want to see Dad's body again.

We walked in. C.J. kept Jude in the lobby. I had decided I didn't want him to see Grandpa Fred in his box.

I was probably projecting my own aversion to the experience onto my son, but in all likelihood, it was also the fact I couldn't fathom watching my son lay his wide blue eyes onto my dad's closed ones. The Missing played the imagined sound of my sweet toddler's voice questioning, *"Grandpa?"*

Nope. No thanks.

I was there for my mother. For the family members who needed the open casket for their own closure. If I could have gotten away with it, I would have stayed in the lobby too, or better yet, I wouldn't have come at all.

Had it been solely up to me, the last memory I would have of my father would be when he was living—singing to me through a computer screen. The Missing lodged itself in my throat.

I approached the casket, obligation driving me forward. The Missing, viciously nipping at my heels herded me up the aisle. I allowed my gaze to rest on my father's body. Waxen. Still. His familiar hands posed on his chest. Glasses on.

"He isn't there," they said. "It's just an empty shell. It's not him."

True.

But the arms that hugged me were there. The hands that made the gravy, even just this past Christmas, and held my son, were there. The green eyes that filled with tears as he preached, they were closed, but they were there. The feet that walked me down the aisle—well, you get the point.

The malignant tumors were also there. I was glad that those were gone and buried deep in the ground—no longer fed by a beating heart.

I think sometimes we dishonor the body of the deceased by saying it's empty when, in fact, it is filled to the brim with sacred memories. Sure, the soul has left, but everything we saw, smelled, touched, and heard is still there, taunting our senses.

It seems for those who've lost loved ones, we have various ways of interacting with the remains. For myself, I chose not to interact at all. I made every effort not to take in anything at the viewing. I do not need an open casket for my own closure. I do, however, understand this is not everyone's preference.

In Mennonite tradition, we bury our dead. We have the casket and the plot of land to take up residency until the end of time. It likely has something to do with the Christian belief of the final resurrection when Jesus comes back, and all of the dead come back to life. Perhaps it's another way we are trying to be considerate of God, making it less work for Him to put us back together—as if anything could be too hard for Him.

I believe cremation is equally sacred and appropriate. In some ways, even more so. From dust we were created, and to dust we return. To be scattered on the wind in a beautiful place sounds lovely. Although not all will be scattered, leaving me to wonder about the number of familial urns passed down through generations that end up in storage lockers.

At the funeral home, we were surrounded by my dad's family. They are a peaceful bunch: kind, gentle, and really funny.

The Missing made the rounds, flamboyantly working the room, relishing all of the attention it was getting.

It draped its arm around my grandpa's shoulders as I leaned down to greet him in his chair with a hug. If I closed my eyes, his hugs felt just like Dad's—soft, with lots of back-patting and bristly kisses.

I couldn't even look at my Uncle Ger because the Missing was projecting the illusion that he was the spitting image of Dad. They'd always looked similar to be sure—Mario and Luigi, we called them. Dad, the shorter and rounder mustached brother, and Ger, the taller and lankier one.

Dad's sisters were teary eyed and loving. My uncles dropped just the right amount of tension-diffusing humor.

Then Dad's friends who'd driven from Wichita walked in. It was my undoing to see the people Dad had ministered with for years. It was weird to see them without Dad among them, animated and lively.

I was thankful for my pregnant belly and the excuse to conveniently slip away to the restroom more times than what would have been socially acceptable. I was glad to take a second to gather my wits—a break from the stench wafting off of the Missing and seeping up the inside of my nose.

Lilies and formaldehyde.

## MOONLIGHT

Finally leaving the funeral home, I gulped in the fresh air like a thirsty marathon runner guzzling water from those tiny paper cups. I took deep, lung-filling breaths for the first time that day. My head pounded from both crying and trying not to cry.

The moon was full and bright, bouncing off the snowy ground and painting the world in silver.

It was nice to see something so beautiful. At the same time, how dare it glow so audaciously.

The Missing unfolded from its stoop and stood tall, stretching to its full height—easily holding the moon in its palm. It reminded me Dad was the one who had first pointed out the moon to Jude. Spinning images with its fingers, projecting them onto the black, starlit screen, the Missing took me back to that day in Kansas when the same moon hung in the clear, blue sky.

That's one of the things I miss about the prairies. Even with its absence of trees and hills and mountains, there is a whole lot of sky. It's as if when God was creating the prairies, he kept unrolling them like wrapping paper—bringing the sky along with them. Horizon to horizon.

That clear winter day beneath the endless sky—a lifetime ago, yet crystal clear in my memory—Jude sat high atop Dad's solid shoulders. In one hand, he firmly grasped Jude's toddler feet and with the other pointed. Jude's gaze followed where his grandpa's index finger indicated the tiny fingernail clipping of a moon against a bright blue backdrop.

"That's the moon, Jude-boy!" he'd said.

"Moon," my towheaded boy repeated. With a drawn-out *oooooo* and a hard /N/ on the end. From that day on, Jude could spot the moon at any given moment. From a moving car window peeking between trees and buildings and telephone poles in any one of its phases.

"Have you gotten around to showing Jude the moon at night yet?" Dad kept asking over the phone. I always put Jude to bed really early so he usually missed the moon's peak viewing, but Dad kept pestering. Sure enough, it blew his little mind the first time he'd witnessed it full and bright in its nighttime splendor—because isn't it only against the backdrop of darkness that anything can really glow?

Now the moon glowed bright and brazenly. The darkness was suffocating, so I turned my face toward the glow of the moon, willing its light to ease the weight of the Missing. The enormity of the next day loomed before me—huge and heavy. I didn't know how I was going to survive it.

The moonlight lit up my feet. There were no footprints to step in this time; I must make my own—one foot in front of the other. The rhythm of my steps in the snow seemed to sing in melancholy baritone:

*Lord, help me today, show me the way, one day at a time.*

*I tried to run away, but the Missing followed my every move. It was wild and unpredictable. It was everywhere at once. It was as fast as the wind when I tried to outrun it, and with a hound nose, it easily found me when I tried to hide. It seemed to know my actions before I did. It was more than a shadow. I wore it. It was a cloak of thick oil, but no matter how hard I scrubbed, the slimy feeling only spread. The places that once brought me solace became unbearable. It tainted everything good and beautiful.*

*The Missing was enormous.*

*It swelled and bloated in size to fill every inch of space, pinning me into a corner. Stretching itself across my vision, it filtered the world with a sick pallor. My eyes only saw the Missing.*

*It could be microscopic.*

*It was too small to pick up between finger and thumb or flick away like a crumb. It climbed down my throat and expanded, lodging itself as a perpetual lump that blocked my air until I released it through tear ducts or choked sobs. It made its way through my digestive system and became a persistent nausea. My heart kept time with the throbbing pain.*

## CHAPTER 4

# The Missing's Funeral

The next morning, my pregnant body rebelled against getting out of bed. The steady diet of *faspa*, the Mennonite word for sandwich trays laden with bread and cheese, had done nothing to help my crowded pregnant intestines. At nearly seven months along, I was now well used to the many aches, pains, and discomforts that come with pregnancy.

Jude was already awake, and I was attempting to pacify him with cartoons, anything to delay having to interact with the day ahead.

It was to decide what to wear for the funeral. My rounded belly limited my options, so stretchy leggings and a brown dress it was. I was glad I had a darker hued option that fit. Although wearing black felt wrong at a "*celebration of life,*" wearing pastels also seemed inappropriate.

Brown felt right. Like dirt.

I still have what I wore that day in my closet. I haven't been able to bring myself to give it away, or ever wear it again. It just hangs there, taking up space.

I was glad the decision about my wardrobe had been simple. Planning a funeral is a million impossible small decisions. Just a few days before I'd sat, legs crossed, on my mom and dad's bed trying to decide what Dad would wear.

Before minimalism was even trendy, there was my dad. There wasn't much to choose from in his meager closet. Every piece of his clothing was well worn; its fabric washed into thin, buttery softness.

The Missing sprawled on Dad's side of the bed, touching every one of his belongings and leaving behind oily fingerprints.

My mom's practical side butted heads against the ritual. *Why bury a perfectly good suit jacket?*

She was already pulling out Dad's clothing and setting it in a pile to be donated to the Siloam Mission that provided for the many homeless in Winnipeg. Dad had spent a lot of time there, meeting with the homeless. He knew them by name. He knew their stories. It was a comforting thought that the few sweaters Dad owned would be given to someone as an added barrier against the Winnipeg winters. That's exactly as Dad would have wanted it.

We chose a suit jacket and jeans. Mom expressed concern that Dad would be "cold," so we added his long johns to the bag to be taken to the funeral home. We emptied his pockets of wadded tissues and receipts.

I tried not to think of the hands that had put them there. I tried not to think of the simple gold wedding band Dad had worn faithfully on his left ring finger. I tried not to think of the shape of his fingernails, the dark hair on his knuckles, and the faint scarring from where our water heater had exploded a little and burned him. I tried not to think of his fingernails with their ever-present semi-circle of car grease. I tried not to think of how his hand felt holding mine while on a walk or in prayer. I tried not to remember the catch in my spirit when I noticed his usual calluses growing smooth from lack of use and too much sitting in his chair by the window. But no matter how hard I tried, that's all the Missing seemed to want to focus on in that moment.

I would never again see those hands.

I tucked the eulogy I had written into my Bible and mentally walked through the day ahead of me. I packed activities and snacks for Jude in his little Elmo backpack and wondered if he would manage to sit through the service. It wasn't going to be brief. Short and sweet is not our family's style.

In some ways, it felt like maybe if we prolonged the service, we were delaying the goodbye. Or maybe we were completely clueless as to how to put together this "Celebration of Life." There had been no prior discussion about funeral arrangements. With Mom clinging so tightly to the belief that Dad would live, there had been no planning of the logistics ahead of time.

We were winging it, and with the guidance of the kind, young pastor of Mom and Dad's tiny congregation, we put something together.

We knew Dad had loved praise and worship. So, we enlisted the praise band from the nearby Spanish congregation to lead us in worship. They had known Dad well, many of them attending Eden B, a theological institute for Spanish-speaking urban leaders.

Putting together the song list turned into a bit of an ordeal. So many songs reflected Dad to us that cutting any one of them felt impossible. So, today we would sing way too many songs. It felt characteristic of Dad to make his funeral similar to a drawn-out church service.

The week before he passed away, he went to his church for the last time. In the middle of the singing, he stood up and left his seat. He shuffled forward to the front of the church. Unable to speak, he turned around to face the congregation. He lifted his hands, his face beseeching. Tears were streaming down his sloping face. Mom was unsure what he was trying to communicate. To her, it looked like he was asking for prayer. He seemed to be saying, *"Remember me in your prayers."* Or maybe he was saying goodbye.

A final benediction from a pastor.

For the service, my younger brother Marcus, who is a musician in San Francisco, and I would sing our rendition of Leonard Cohen's "Hallelujah." Marcus had played it recently for my dad through the phone, and Dad had really liked it. The Missing hummed the haunting chorus in my ear.

Marcus and I played and sang together in church a lot as teenagers. Marcus is something of a musical phenom. In piano recitals growing up, he would get up there and blow everyone away, earning a standing ovation from a previously sleepy audience. Then, it was my turn to follow his performance with whatever mediocre talent I could pull together.

My musical skills are sufficient at best. Still, practicing the song in my parents' living room felt like putting on a comfortable pair of well-worn shoes: familiar and with the right amount of nostalgia to carry me through.

I love singing with Marcus.

Marcus is tall, brilliant, and hilarious. He tends to say what he's thinking, and usually what he's thinking is incredibly clever and quirky. He once, at my mother-in-law's formal Christmas dinner table, posed the sincere question to everyone there: "When was the time that you were most afraid for your life?" My bite of holiday supper nearly sprayed all over the fancy cloth placemats.

It came time to leave for the funeral. C.J. and I loaded Jude into our rental car. The service would take place in a church we'd never been to. Dad was well-loved, and the church he and mom attended would not be able to fit the number of people we expected to be there.

Crossing over the Disraeli Bridge that spans the mighty Red River, I spotted the hearse.

The Missing let out an exclamation and delivered me a punch to the gut.

I immediately knew it was Dad.

C.J. fell silent as he noticed it too. We ended up following directly behind it the entire 20-minute drive to the church. I think we hit every stoplight on the way there.

Barely able to talk, I weakly joked, "I guess Dad wanted to navigate to be sure we didn't get lost."

The Missing roared in my ears. I looked down at my lap so I didn't have to see the unfinished pine box peeking out the back curtains every time we stopped.

When we finally pulled into the parking lot, I breathed a sigh of relief that the hearse was parked on the other end. I wanted to be as far away from it as possible.

## A CELEBRATION OF LIFE

Clarence lined us up behind the casket.

The Missing took me back to the processional before my own wedding. We stood in a line outside the chapel. I was standing in my big white dress that I'd been so excited to have found on clearance. I held my dad's arm. We listened for the music that would cue my big entrance.

He shifted his weight from side to side and clenched his jaw to try to keep from getting choked up. Tears were common for Dad, and his tears were inevitable that day. It wasn't a matter of *if* he would cry, it was a matter of when. Along with walking me down the aisle, we had asked him to officiate the vows.

The beautiful piano music swelled, and Dad and I took our steps down that center aisle. Our friends and family rose to their feet, huge smiles on their faces. I looked amazing and couldn't wait to marry the young man waiting for me at the front of the church. We made it through the giving away of the bride part. Dad kept a steady, assured voice as he said his line,

"Her mother and I do."

The all too familiar voice crack I had been anticipating ended up happening when he asked me if I took C.J. to be my husband.

I'm not sure what it was about that particular moment or the word *"husband"* that struck a nerve and conjured emotion for my Dad. Perhaps it was because he knew the profound responsibility and weight that came with being a husband and having a husband. Perhaps he was remembering his own vows.

The vows we chose to speak that day were the same words that Dad and Mom spoke to one another in the Hillsboro, Kansas MB church in 1977. C.J. and I decided to speak the traditional vows to one another after Dad explained to us that every time he heard those same vows while attending another wedding, he relived the moment that he proclaimed those words to Mom. I loved that.

I doubt when Mom vowed to love Dad in *"sickness and in health,"* she had any idea what she was agreeing to. How often she must have revisited that promise. When Dad was stripped of his faculties and didn't even know who she was; when his brain was tricking him into saying some bizarre and terrifying things; when she held him as he seized—with every spoon-fed bite, she walked out those vows.

I don't know what is in store for C.J and me. I don't know how thin those vows will be stretched. I don't know how much more of the worse we will see than the better, what ratio of sickness to health we will experience, if the poorer will be more prevalent than the richer. On a wedding day, so much is unknown. But that day, in front of my dad and God and a full church with a center aisle, I made that promise. And with that promise, we took that step into the unknown future.

But this center aisle did not lead to a picturesque scene framing a smiling lovestruck couple. This center aisle was flanked by the weeping, the distressed, and the devastated. *Why did they stand as we entered?* Better they would sit so I wouldn't have to be face-level with so many teary eyes.

As the song, "I Will Rise" played, the Missing sat heavily on my feet, and I heaved them forward one step at a time. I clutched C.J.'s arm with one hand and the Elmo backpack with his red, mocking smile in the other. We somehow made it up the aisle to our reserved pew to the left.

Dad's coffin sat in the front of the church. Instead of a large flower arrangement that didn't make any sense for him, Clarence had suggested we leave his bible open on top, along with a framed photograph and a wooden sculpture Dad had made. Every so often Dad would feel urges to create. This particular wooden sculpture is symbolic of the Holy Trinity with a cross, a bird, and a blue circle attached together. Made with his hands.

His strong, capable hands. Hands with their hairy knuckles, grease-darkened crescent moon fingernails, and gold ring.

The congregational singing began. I tried to choke out the lyrics, but the Missing had its hand around my throat and was roaring Dad's voice into my eardrums so all I could hear was the missing baritone voice that loved to belt out these songs.

Everyone was so sad.

It is really hard to sing praise and worship songs to God when you are so sad. I wasn't even sure if God and I were on speaking terms at that moment, and I could find very little to worship Him about. Oh, how I wished we'd cut out some of these songs.

Mom lifted her arms and waved them, trying to get the crowd to join in and celebrate that Dad was now whole and healed and in the presence of the Most High.

Some people tried to oblige by clapping slightly off-beat before petering out awkwardly.

When it came time for Marcus and me to sing our song, I went numb and closed my eyes. I took comfort in finding the harmonies we had practiced.

A broken hallelujah, fittingly so.

The four children of the deceased approached the pulpit. I read the eulogy.

It was probably the many drama classes I had taken in high school and college that helped me keep the Missing from dissolving me in a bucket of my own tears. It was also likely due to the many indulgent meltdowns I'd allowed myself to have in the days leading up to this point—absorbing my sobs in my pillow or taking turns with my family to be the crier in the room.

I've discovered that if I can allow the tears to freely fall and the sobs to punch with their full sound at times when I am in a secure place, I can control my emotions better when out in public—like those controlled burns that are intentionally started to stop the entire forest from burning down.

I'd indulged the Missing more than enough controlled burns up to this point, so today, I could retreat to a numb, stoic place and keep my composure through the song and reading. Barely.

Jude soon got antsy and bored with his activities. Uncle Kevin made silly faces in the pew behind us to keep him entertained.

Finally, the service ended. At Clarence's gentle cue, we filed back up the center aisle.

My *delicate* state had excused me from being one of the pallbearers. That honor went to my siblings and their spouses. I was glad I didn't have to be near the casket.

It's a confusing thing to find something horrifically repulsive and yet impossibly sacred all at once. The Missing held both sides of the magnet. I was both drawn in and repelled. I wanted nothing to do with the big pine box, and yet I dreaded the moment it would disappear into the earth.

## THE BURIAL

Closing the door to our rental car with only myself, C.J., and an overtired Jude felt like something akin to relief. Perhaps the Missing carpooled with someone else. It was a respite from the small talk, the condolences, and the reverberating "I'm praying for you."

Every time someone says, "Well, I'll pray for you," I can't help but think it's more like something Christians say to end the conversation or to thank someone for the information. I'm often skeptical people *will* actually pray for you when you're not standing directly in front of them.

We pointed our GPS to Nivervilleto the small cemetery. I'd taken the same highway route hundreds of times before. The small Bible college I'd attended is just a few miles south of Dad's burial plot.

My dad had been the one to drive me to college. As a former convent, it has an impressive bell tower that is visible for miles across the open prairies before you actually arrive at the campus. As a 19-year-old who had never lived away from home, the sight of it threw me into a panic. Dad held my hand and launched into prayer over me. For peace, for courage—believing there were good things in store for me there. And there were.

Rarely did I hear Dad say the words, "I'll pray for you." He would typically pray then and there. He tended to live life in the moment.

He helped me move into my dorm room and snapped a picture of me and my roommate for my mom. It made him happy and proud that I would be attending college mere miles from the place of his birth, our roots entwined in circular patterns.

Now he would be buried among those same roots.

Gazing out the passenger side window, I snacked on a protein bar and chugged some water. I would have forgotten had it not been for the squirmy reminder in my belly. I'd visited my obstetrician the day before boarding my flight to Winnipeg. I wanted to be sure everything was good with the baby before I dove head-first into pain and trauma.

"*You must* remember to eat," she had reminded me with empathic tear-filled eyes. Despite the violence of the Missing, Lyla Rae was still coming. Even in the midst of my grief, I still counted as two. Any selfishness I felt must have its limits.

It was a beautiful day. The prairie skies were bright blue, contrasting sharply with the white early spring snow still deciding whether to melt or not. The sun was the only thing that seemed to do anything to offset the chill of the Missing. It was surprising to me that it wasn't gloomy and raining. The weather was a peculiar paradox.

We pulled into the small cemetery. Clarence and his hearse were already there. A rectangle was sliced out of the frozen ground, a carpet of green Astroturf framed it.

My dad's sister had come up with the thoughtful idea of writing messages on the casket before it was buried. She passed out markers. Jude, thrilled to have been given an activity, immediately yanked the lid off of a green one and cavalierly made a long scribble down the side of the casket, like he was keying a car.

"There!" he said. "That's better."

*That's better.* I approached the casket with my own marker, wracking my brain for the words. *What could I possibly write? Could I write anything that could possibly make it 'better'?*

While Mom and Dad were never big on gifts, they loved writing long messages in our birthday cards. They always signed it separately. They would share Bible verses they prayed for me and the hopes and blessings they had for me. Dad's handwriting was always a little hard to decipher, but the thought and time he put into each and every birthday card was a gift in itself.

In my last birthday card from Dad, in a shaky, unfamiliar hand and tiny letters, I could barely make out the words, *"Love, Dad."* In Mom's birthday card just a few days after mine, Dad had managed to draw only the tiniest of hearts.

Love was the last thing to fade.

My hand hovered over the box. I tried not to picture him beneath the lid. I finally wrote something hopelessly generic about heaven and signed it, *"Your Beauty."*

He'd always called me *"Beauty."*

I can't remember the song we sang around the grave. Grandpa, who'd been a choir conductor for many years, led the song over his son with a sad strength. Tearful harmonies surrounded the rectangle with the pine box hovering above it, draped in loved-ones' scribbled messages.

My body hurt. The sides of my belly stretched painfully, and my feet swelled in my boots. The Missing pulled me into its orbit. I was heavy with exhausted gravity.

Suddenly it was time to step away from the green rectangle and go back to our car. There was part of me that wanted to sprint away and never look back. Still, another part of me wanted to fling myself on top of the casket and scream. I wanted to cling to it like a bug on a windshield until my family had to scrape me off of it.

But Jude. My boy.

The only grandchild of the departed. Blissfully unaware of the finality of the Missing, he was watching his mama. I must not be indulgent in my grief.

I opted to silently approach the casket and touch the lid above where I imagined Dad's face to be. I kissed my fingertips and touched it again.

"I love you Dad," I said to the wood.

*Abba, I belong to You.*

In that moment, I felt every bit my daddy's girl and every bit fatherless.

The hope of heaven didn't seem to be enough. I turned away from the repulsive, precious box. The Missing danced around me in a frenzied dervish dance.

Back in the silence of the car, we pulled out of the cemetery. I looked back. One more look before my daddy was lowered into the ground. We had opted not to watch, and I'm glad for that. I don't know how I could have endured standing there as the pine box disappeared from the surface of the earth to be planted in the dirt, among the worms and cold and darkness becoming one with his roots.

Clarence had said he would take care of it, and I knew he would.

The combination of bright sun and white snow blinded me. Clarence stood post next to the hole in the earth. He was St. Peter ushering Dad through heaven's gates. He would be the one to do the lowering. To draw the muddy veil. To cover.

My mental reel of this scene is pure, blinding white: white hair, white mustache, and white snow. Everything was lit up in its transcendent glow. Beautiful and holy. Sacred and solemn. Ethereal.

The Missing flung its arms wide, fully embracing its liberation. It would not be staying there in the graveyard. No, it was already blowing freely across the plains—loose and wild. And although this torturous day was now over, the Missing was in the prime of its youth; its journey had only just begun.

*It was a quicksand growing deeper by the second. The more I struggled, the deeper I sank.*

*My mind floated in a pool of the Missing's presence. Not the kind of effortless floating that happens in calm waters where you lay back and stare at the sky, ears submerged in silence—but frantic egg-beater legs and arms, all too aware of the deep, dark depths just below and desperate not to be sucked down into them.*

*My body physically ached from the exhaustion of sheer survival. Living was something I had done before. Before the Missing. Before the unfair exchange. One presence for another.*

*I traded living for surviving.*

## CHAPTER 5

# The Missing and a Baby

Jude and I stayed with my mom through Easter. On Easter Sunday, we went to the small church my parents had attended and served at for years. I hid in the kid's playroom with Jude. The Missing was sharp and painful in that space. It wanted to lurch me back to the funeral—to the singing that wouldn't end.

By the time we flew home, the daffodils and tulips were poking up out of the soggy ground. The fact that Dad died the week before Easter is the only thing that makes sense to me about his death. As his family, we never doubted his love for us. But the message of Jesus is what drove Dad. He was always Dad's first love.

Early in our marriage, Dad came to speak at one of our jr. high fall retreats. He stood at the front of a small chapel nestled in the woods and told a room full of preteens to hold their arms up in front of them—elbow meeting elbow, forming a cross with their forearms.

"The cross is your covering," he'd told them. And that's how he'd lived—moving cross-first through the world.

Even today, while the message of Easter is supposed to be about only Jesus, my thoughts always return to Dad. I can't help but picture him holding up his hairy forearms in front of him—choking up as he often did when he spoke of the crucifixion of

Jesus. Willing the room full of young kids with teary eyes to love Jesus as he did.

Leaving mom was hard. To watch her sit alone in church, she seemed as if she had been split in half.

"I have Jesus," she reassured me. But all I saw was the Missing in my father's seat next to her.

I felt like I was abandoning her to the abuse of the Missing. Knowing my sister was there made me feel better, but in some ways, it would be the broken taking care of the broken. The lost guiding the lost. Together they would stumble into the fog of the Missing in search of their new normal; their lives were no longer tangled up in doctor appointments and hospital waiting rooms.

We were all fumbling forward into the *'after.'* It was our own A.D.—After Death.

Jude and I arrived home to C.J. and a mantle full of sympathy cards. Our church rallied around me with meals and prayers. C.J. surprised me with the nursery being freshly painted. He and a group of dear friends had banded together to cover the unfortunate beige with a soft and serene gray, ready to be turned into the girly nursery of my dreams.

Whether I was ready or not, it was time to start thinking about the next major life event soon to come.

The theme for my sweet Lyla Rae's nursery was *'feminine with a little bit of whimsy'* and designing it was my happy place. When the Missing talked too much, I turned away from it and applied my thoughts to decorating—scrolling Pinterest for inspiration, and unearthing tiny porcelain teacups and china dolls from my own precious box of childhood treasures that I had carefully squirreled away.

During that time of "nesting," my rambunctious Jude tried to scale the dresser we'd bought for the nursery, and it came toppling over on top of him.

I quickly scooped him up and assessed him. He was un-scathed, but we noticed one of my porcelain boxes was shattered. Jude immediately melted down because he broke one of Lyla's "pretty boxes." I shushed him and held him, and I tried not to let him see the tears that burned my eyes.

It was just a thing.

It had no soul or spirit. It served no real purpose or function, beyond putting other tiny, special things inside of it. But it was a piece of my past: a treasure from the room of my childhood. A room that I had long since vacated and was now filled with new inhabitants and new experiences. "Laura's room" no longer existed. It was now only a place in the timeline of my memories.

The rooms of my childhood were my haven. It was the place where I would read and recharge, where I painted my nails and memorized my pores in the mirror before pimples were even a threat. I was fortunate not to have to share a room for the majority of my childhood. I think my parents understood the importance of me having my own space. There was my room in L.A. with the tulip wallpaper, and then my room in Wichita in which my parents allowed me to paint an amateur watercolor mural of roses and butterflies. Eventually, we sponge-painted over it with blue and white so that it looked like clouds.

Everything I have managed to keep from my childhood carries a substantial amount of sentiment for me. Since the haul is quite meager, each item carries for me worth well beyond what is practical. Nothing I had in my possession as a child was frivolous to me—even the teacups too small to ever hold liquid. I attached meaning to everything.

I still do.

Thus, the breaking of a porcelain box with bunnies on it was my undoing. When Jude eventually moved on to something else leaving me to clean up the glass, the Missing blew in with exaggerated emotion laced with hormones.

I picked up the shattered porcelain pieces and wept like an orphan. I wept over the rooms of my childhood. I wept over the young girl I had been.

## THE ROBBERY

A few weeks before Lyla's due date, C.J. and I arrived home to find every drawer and cabinet wide open. We'd been robbed.

Our pillowcases had been stripped from our beds and filled with our possessions before being removed. Jude's dresser drawers had been rifled through, and my perfect girly nursery had been touched by a stranger's hands.

Along with our game system, some other odds and ends, and, randomly, even the juice in our fridge—they stole C.J.'s gold wedding band. He'd left it on our dresser for safekeeping while he went to the gym. Ironically, he took it off so it *wouldn't* get stolen. The gold band he'd thoughtfully chosen. The yellow gold band that did not match my white gold engagement and wedding rings.

"Can we do that?" I'd asked him as a young, naive bride-to-be. It had never even crossed my mind that our wedding bands wouldn't match.

His answer was true to who he is. He is forever thinking outside the box in thoughtful and non-conforming ways. He explained to me that all of the men in his life he would consider his spiritual role models and men he could look up to as godly husbands had simple, yellow gold wedding bands—Dad included. I loved that.

Before we were married, I'd had our wedding date engraved on the inside of it along with the words *Love Endures*.

In the *"better or worse"* part of our vows, getting robbed certainly felt like *"worse."* This actually wasn't even the first time C.J. and I had experienced this. At the end of our honeymoon week on the way to the airport, we stopped at a waterfall. While we were away from our rental Jeep, someone had stolen our suitcases from inside of it. I flew home with nothing but a chapstick in my pocket. That was my first big lesson in holding all things loosely. Nothing in this world is permanent. Don't cling to possessions.

I remember one night as a child; a man came to the door. He held a gun to my father and ordered him to give up anything of value. He directed my dad through the house while my mom hid under her bed covers and prayed. The rest of us were asleep upstairs. Although Dad would have quickly and easily given over anything worth any significant amount of money, we had very little to give the robber.

We were most upset about the VCR he took with him. Mom had saved from her grocery budget for months to purchase it.

Staring at my son's open dresser drawers, I thought about the hands rifling through his pajamas. The violation cut through me. The Missing filled my home up from the floor to the ceiling. With every fresh realization of another thing the thief had stolen, I felt the robbing of something much bigger.

I felt the violation of the Missing.

The hollow emptiness of what had been stolen from me.

Nothing felt safe.

Our home had been ransacked. All of our belongings had been gone through and touched. Aside from our sense of security, it was the loss of C.J.'s wedding band that stung the most.

Gone was the tangible symbol for our marital commitment, and it was a fitting metaphor for the lack of safety I was feeling even in my relationship with C.J. Oh, he was loving and present, but he now was married to another: "America the Beautiful," herself.

She owned him, this mistress of patriotism. *Did his vow to her now come before his vow to me?* I wasn't sure how it all worked. I fantasized about calling the President himself or crafting an especially moving letter to mail off to 1600 Pennsylvania Avenue in which I would plead my case and ask if it were possible for them to postpone my husband's impending orders until I was emotionally ready. *Would he consider staying my marriage's execution?*

The Missing snidely waved a tiny American flag with one hand and played the world's tiniest violin with the other—no sympathy here.

And I wondered: *Could our love endure even this?*

Along with the lack of safety I felt in my home and marriage, another source of my security and reassurance was buried deep in the ground in Canadian prairies. I had been robbed. I was *still* being robbed.

*And God?* I held my heavy arms up in front of me, elbow to elbow, and begged him to cover me.

Being robbed is a violation that takes a while to get over. Grief is the robbery that never ends. The Missing continues to take and take—and then continues to point out what's gone, what's *missing*. Every time I try to explain Grandpa Fred to my kids, I am reminded anew that not only was I robbed—they were too.

## HURRY UP AND WAIT

Military limbo is a place I have come to expect in my short career as a military wife. It's that space of time where you know orders are on their way, but you don't quite have them yet. You are left waiting and wondering. Anyone who has lived the military life can attest—you can't plan anything.

The military has no regard for 'plans. Until you have official orders in hand, you cannot count on anything. From the moment C.J. signed his paperwork, I was once again thrown into the wilderness of the unknown.

I went from Dad's cancerous limbo to a red, white, and blue limbo where the answer to each and every question posed to me was,

"I don't know."

"Will C.J. be there for the birth?"

"I don't know."

"Where is he going?"

"I don't know."

"Will he be home for Christmas?"

"I don't know."

I don't know. I don't know. I don't know. It's really hard not knowing, *you know?*

I plodded forward, keeping my eyes on my swollen ankles. If I tried to look further ahead than what was *today*, all I saw was the dark mist of the Missing swallowing up my future.

Finally, we received orders that said C.J. was to report for Officer Candidate School (OCS) exactly one month following Lyla's due date. We were relieved to know he would at least be present for the birth.

As my due date approached, so did the date for C.J.'s departure.

Jude and I spent much of that summer in the neighborhood swimming pool. It was my one relief from the heaviness—heaviness of my body and heaviness of my spirit. I floated easily. My pregnant belly, buoyant and huge, protruded from the surface of the water as I submerged my ears in the silence allowing my limbs to drift upward in the cool water—dangling weightlessly.

Jude made his pudgy toddler hands into circles and held them to his eyes,

"There it is! The white whale!"

Never does time move more slowly than for a mother in her last month of pregnancy. Along with the typical overall feeling of being 'done' with being uncomfortably enormous, I felt another layer of urgency. *Maybe if I could get Lyla here sooner rather than later, I could have more time with C.J. here to help?* There would be more time for Jude to adjust to life with a little sister before his Daddy was whoosh—missing.

We could have at least one solid month of our new normal before it changed again.

As any mother who has given birth knows, babies have a mind of their own even in utero and Lyla had no intention of coming early—although she gave me plenty of practice contractions that got my hopes up.

I was eager to move into the next stage of my healing.

My general experience with postpartum pain is it's a hopeful type of pain. It is reasonable to expect that in a week, you will at least physically feel better than you do at that moment, and in another week, you'll feel better again—and so on.

I thought that's how it would be when Dad died. I thought that the healing would be more linear. That each day would be subsequently easier than the day before. I remember asking a dear friend of mine who'd lost her dad,

"When does it get better?"

I wanted a number. A time frame.

The day he died I thought, *Well, it's over. This is as bad as it's going to get. It's all uphill from here.*

Or is it downhill? I am never quite sure which direction is best. Going uphill is challenging, whereas going downhill, gravity helps you along. Then again, up is good, and down is bad.

Either way, I was wrong. The day that Dad died wasn't the worst it would get. The worst was when the Missing became a constant fixture in my life, and I was confronted with the permanence. It's the permanence of the Missing that is the most devastating.

Everything hurt. My body hurt. My heart hurt.

I just wanted to get better.

But as my wonderful pastor gently put it to me, "To say you want to get better implies that there's something wrong with you. You're not sick. You're not broken. You're grieving."

I suppose part of me thought that if I could be done with the pregnancy part of the hard and move into the hopeful postpartum phase of healing, maybe all of me would feel better. I suppose I'd also forgotten how hard the postpartum phase could be.

## THE PULL OF THE MOON

On July 21, 2013, I began to have strong, legitimate, perfectly respectable contractions in the evening. I clocked them with an app on my phone wondering if this was the real deal. But they never got any stronger or closer together and finally fizzled out.

I swore at the Duchess of Cambridge after midnight when I saw on the glowing television that she was in the hospital in active labor with Prince George.

Damn her and her perfect hair and her gaggle of nannies!

Switching off the television, I sat in the darkness by the window. The moon glowed huge and full once again.

The silvery moonlight drew me back to the funeral home, to the smell of formaldehyde and lilies. My son perched high on Dad's shoulders pointing at the sky and smiling his huge toothy grin. Dad's hands, gold wedding band in place, encircling Velcro shoes—holding secure and tight.

The gravity of the Missing drew me into its orbit.

My mental reel began to play—slouchy smile, warm hand, gaping mouth, pine box, closed eyes, white snow.

*I don't want to go in there.*

Untethered, I drifted further into the panicky darkness of the Missing, sucked into the infinite, airless oblivion until with a jolt I stopped myself.

*Lyla.*

My girl was there too. *Could she feel my heart racing? Did she wonder why her snug, spherical bed felt tighter with the squeeze of sobs mixing with contractions?*

*Abba, I belong to You. Abba, I belong to You. Abba, I belong to You.*

I breathed my prayer into an imaginative paper bag until the hyperventilating slowed and the moonlight stopped burning my skin.

I even dared to pray for Princess Kate once I'd finished swearing at her.

I finally trudged back to my bedroom where my husband slept in peaceful ignorance. I tried not to think about how in a month's time that side of the bed would be empty. The Missing, albeit in a different way, would be coming for him too.

## ARRIVAL

When the sun went down and the full moon rose out of the horizon the next night, the sporadic contractions started up again. Again, I clocked them with my phone and contended with the Missing, who preened ostentatiously amidst the collision of my physical labor pains and emotional anguish given new intensity by the light of the silvery moon.

I thought about what it must have been like for Jacob to wrestle the angel.

*"I won't let go until you've blessed me."*

*"I won't let go until you get this baby out of me!"*

When the sun came up, I was exhausted. Two nights of sleepless contractions combined with the weariness that comes with relentless missing.

Thankfully, my mom arrived that day.

I set her up in our unfinished basement. The Missing perched on her shoulders. She cried easily. I tiptoed around her feelings and gave whatever I had left to seek to bring her comfort.

In some ways at that time, I felt as though the Missing had stolen both of my parents.

Upon learning I'd spent two nights up with contractions, my doctor sent me to the hospital to get checked out.

They checked me out, and then checked me in.

I called my mom and told her to come to us at the hospital as soon as my mother-in-law could get there to watch Jude.

C.J. and I had discussed it earlier and decided my mom would be in the room when her namesake was born. Having spent much of the last season of her life in the depression of hospitals with Dad, I thought maybe experiencing something happy in a hospital could be a good thing.

For myself as well. Even being there in active labor, the Missing kept interrupting with memories of the hospital in Winnipeg.

Sure, this was a completely different hospital. A different state. A different country even. But there is a universal hospital smell—antiseptic and urine—even the texture of the hospital gown drew me back to that hospital a thousand miles north.

Seven hours after getting checked in, Lyla Rae was born. On her due date.

'Lyla,' means darkness, or night. 'Rae,' means ewe or sheep. She would be my lamb in the darkest of seasons. My full moon against the night sky.

My mom shrieked with laughter as Lyla emerged. My mom has a great laugh—like a bird. A bird that starts with a loud burst on an upper octave and then vibrates. On July 23, 2013, Mom laughed her high pitch bird song laugh, even as tears streamed down her face. Armed with her camera, she followed the nurses around the room with excited exclamations of joy.

"Don't put that hat on her head! She has such beautiful hair!" We later learned that the hat does serve an actual purpose in keeping the newborn babe warm. It's not just for cuteness. The sweet nurses accommodated the shrieking Grandma anyway and left Lyla's boastfully round, wet head exposed.

In that brief moment, it felt as though maybe hospitals had been redeemed. Joy filled that moment from top to bottom, and I cried tears of relief that the pregnancy was over and my perfect little girl was here. *Maybe now we could crowd the Missing out with the purest of joys? Maybe the innocence of my little girl's presence would drive out the darkest night? Maybe we'd finally won this battle against suffering and taken a step toward actual healing?*

The Missing stepped forward for its turn to hold the baby. My heart sank deep into my empty belly, and I knew that—clutch her tightly though I might— I must eventually relinquish the swaddled bundle.

The Missing cradled her gently. Its face leaned into my newborn's furrowed brow, and in a raspy baritone it began to sing an eerie lullaby of one refrain—"*If only if only if only.*" It rocked back and forth, back and forth.

It became clear to me as the Missing's breath misted over my daughter's perfect sleeping face—I couldn't protect her. No matter how hard I tried, the Missing would be there for her too. It wasn't going anywhere.

*I longed for a reprieve. I craved sleep that seldom came.*

*Nightly, the Missing sat beside my bed and projected the most traumatic of my memories on the ceiling above my bed. From the uselessness of my pillow, I relived the worst of my mental reel again and again and again. The sound of dying. The smell of death. The violent taking. The empty warmth would turn cold.*

*In my mind, I walked the halls of the funeral home. The hospital. The phone conversations that brought pain. The feeling of broken earth beneath my feet. The tearing away. The guilt that came with the relief of it being 'over'.*

*Even the moon brought pain because it had dared to shine beautifully over the most heinous of nights. I resented its audacious constancy.*

*If sleep came, the Missing followed me into my dreams. It teased me with visions of what had been or could have been. The only thing real about the dreams were the tears on my cheeks when I finally awoke—punctuated with a painful jolt of fresh reality.*

## CHAPTER 6

# The Missing Joins the Military

I've always been hopelessly romantic. As a child, I romanticized everything and was quite a proficient daydreamer. I stole away into my mind frequently and with vivid detail.

Typically, in my daydreams, I would leave the confines of the city where there were houses stacked on houses. It was noisy and crowded, divided by chain link and iron fences; helicopters and cars vibrated to the beat of their cranked-up bass.

In the privacy of my mind, I was in wide open fields with horses and wildflowers. There were never any mosquitos, and the breeze would blow my hair in a flattering way before the sky would open up with the warmest of rains. For some reason, there would always be a handsome boy in that field to lock eyes with. He would tuck a wildflower behind my ear, and then with innocent progression, we would hold hands under the stars.

The romantic fuzzies followed me into adolescence. I would have crushes on boys and daydream about them daydreaming about me. In my imagination, the possibility of romance was endless. I was graceful and mysteriously fascinating. In reality, I was awkward and reserved. If I thought a boy was cute, I ignored him. I would clam up and never speak to him.

That was until C.J.

He and I never had trouble talking to one another.

We met in high school choir class our senior year at Heights High School in Wichita, Kansas. The first image I have of him is him smiling as we put our music folders away in their designated slots. I was immediately comfortable with this tall, lanky, clean-cut football player.

His joy was infectious. His mouth was always wide open in chatter and loud laughter. We became fast friends. I loved being around him, and in the deepest corners of my heart where I kept my secrets, I knew I loved him.

He was different from any other guy I'd known. He carried his Bible around with him, but not in a *"look how Christian I am"* attitude that permeated the Evangelical youth culture of those days. It was all new to him. He was not raised in church like I was.

So when I saw him with bags under his eyes falling asleep in class and he told me he'd been up all night reading his Bible and trying to make sense of it, I loved him even more.

He grilled me about my family, especially my dad. For a long time, I thought he only wanted to be around me because he was drawn to my family and wanted to learn more about what a typical Christian family looked like. The joke was on him because although we were Christian, my family was far from typical.

I told myself he didn't love me like I loved him. I wrote poems in my journal about unrequited love once I learned what unrequited meant.

He was my friend. Nothing more.

That is until he held my hand.

Butterflies don't even adequately describe it. It was an entire flock of albatross. Every romantic notion I'd ever dwelled on in the privacy of my imagination was given flight. His hand was strong and large, dwarfing my own and silencing any childhood insecurities I'd ever had about my hands being too big for a girl.

For all my elaborate daydreams, nothing had prepared me for falling in love. It was an experience unlike anything I could have imagined.

He reached for my hand just a couple of weeks before I was to leave for my college on the Canadian prairies one thousand miles away from him. I was all his from that moment on. Our friendship caught fire.

After two years of weekly phone calls, countless emails, and only a smattering of in-person visits when school was on break, he asked my dad if he could marry me. Together they sat on a bed full of laundry to be folded in the tight space of my parent's bedroom. My dad only asked him two questions in response to C.J.'s nervous request.

"Do you feel like that's what Jesus is leading you to do?" and, "What does Laura think?"

C.J.'s answers were good enough for Dad.

I've thought about this over the years. If Dad had any antiquated concern over how C.J. was going to provide for me, he didn't show it. In fact, I doubt it even crossed his mind because he didn't view C.J. as the provider. God was the Provider. Dad's only concern was *who* we were following.


## EXPECTATIONS

The first time I drove onto a military base was in Wichita, Kansas, for C.J.'s swearing-in. As I proceeded past the guard tower with my tow-headed toddler in the backseat, the Missing sat up straight with excited anticipation. It relished the impending dramatic change to come.

I drove the slow speed limit on the base. I had the same feeling that crawls down your back when a highway patrol car is driving directly behind you. Even though you're not doing anything wrong, you plant your hands at ten and two and keep your eyes straight ahead, skittishly glancing at the speedometer every so often.

I drove slowly into an unfamiliar future. A world I had no experience in. The uniforms and acronyms. The way they called me ma'am. It was all so foreign. Ministry was familiar. Ministry I *knew*.

I was supposed to be a minister's wife. Not a military one.

Just weeks before our wedding, when it was time to get in the car and leave home for the last time, Dad pulled me aside for one last heart-to-heart. With tears in his eyes and a hushed intensity he began to ramble,

"I don't think I ever told you, you could be anything you wanted. You could be a doctor, a lawyer—"

I was taken aback by this rare showing of near desperation. I forcefully interrupted his rambling with a strong verbal assurance that I wanted to marry C.J. and begin my life as the wife of a full-time youth minister.

I look back on this and wonder if this was the equivalent of a parental cramming session. Although I was only 21 years old, I felt like the wheels had already been set in motion, and my life was mapped out. I would marry into the ministry. I felt like I knew what I was getting into because my childhood had prepared me. I think it's likely Dad saw how naive I was and wanted to be sure I knew I had all the professional career options in the world. This is ironic to me because Dad himself never even graduated college. He went to a year or two of Bible college in British Columbia before dropping out with bad grades. Shortly after this, he left for L.A. and entered full-time ministry.

Although basic education was a given in my family, my mom and dad put very little emphasis on any of us becoming 'successful' in a career field. They encouraged us to follow our dreams and passions. Thus, I ended up with a non-accredited

Bachelor of Fine Arts in Drama from a small college on the Manitoba prairies.

The thing is, I never wanted to be a doctor or a lawyer. Or really to have anything that could be considered a profession. Toward the end of my childhood, I felt *'called'* into full-time ministry, figuring I must marry someone who also felt the same calling.

It was as simple as that in my mind. Although my life wasn't completely mapped out down to every minute detail, I saw the general framework with perfect clarity. Or so I thought.

I envisioned C.J. and I spending our life doing ministry in one form or another. I would be C.J.'s partner as well as the full-time mother to our children. We would spend our life serving God and discipling others. Our children would have a childhood similar to mine in that they would be children of the church.

My new daydreams of those days were full of C.J. preaching and me playing the piano. I would stand at his side. I would submit like I was supposed to, and he would love me as Christ loved the church and died for it.

Even writing this out now feels so contrived—boxed in.

I click my tongue and shake my head at 21-year-old Laura now. She had no idea what was ahead.

I suppose none of us really do. Life has a way of throwing every one of us curve balls. Though sometimes I fancy myself exceptional, the reality is I'm not.


**DRAFTED**

I sent C.J. home the first night Lyla was born. I told him I would feel better knowing he was with Jude now abruptly thrown into big brotherhood, and it would be good if he got a full night's sleep.

Looking back, it's likely I was already beginning to distance myself from C.J. I didn't understand the world I was about to step into. I didn't understand the dramatic shift of direction in our marriage. I felt certain I needed to stop needing him, and it might as well start the first night of our daughter's life.

The full moon shone through the hospital window and reflected off the clear plastic bassinet that held 8lbs 5ozs of pure sweetness. I had carried her within me, and yet she was a stranger. My thoughts drifted to my round-faced toddler at home. Him I knew. I knew which spoon he ate the best with and that he liked to sleep with water next to his bed. I knew which T.V. shows would keep his attention the longest, which shirt was his favorite, and which ones had scratchy tags. I was the one who knew if he didn't go outside during the day, his bedtime routine would be a struggle. I knew he would be missing me.

I knew him. Just as I thought I had known C.J., but now, with the Missing obscuring my view, I barely recognized him.

The Missing's imposing form stood between the moonlight and my hospital bed sending shadow puppets onto the white cotton sheets. It contorted its spidery hands into shapes projecting shadows of an elaborate scene with military aircraft and ground vehicles. Its sharp, fanning fingernails morphed into rows of marching shadow soldiers. I searched them for C.J., but I was unable to find him amongst the dark, and faceless in uniform. They kept step one after another in black formation against the silvery moonlight background, spiraling around the hospital bed and bassinet until I was surrounded. They grew larger with the sound of the maniacal puppeteer's cackling.

Desperate to curb the anxiety welling up, I reached for the swaddled babe in her clear, plastic manger. Even with the nurse's obligatory warning against co-sleeping fresh in my mind, I pulled Lyla onto the bed with me. I lay on my left side and tucked her back into the place she had been not 24 hours before. My sore, swollen body formed a question mark as it curled around the flannel bundle. I positioned my face as close to her face as I could.

Breathing in the sweet air from her tiny open mouth, my heartbeat slowed. Air from new lungs was activated by pure, helpless, God-given instinct. A new life whose only hardship endured thus far could be quickly remedied by a tight swaddle.

*Abba, I belong to You.*

The Missing rolled its eyes and stuffed its hands back into its pockets. Turning its back to me, it directed its attention back out the window to the full moon; its face was aglow in gray shadow.

## COLIC

I arrived home with a new baby to a master closet taken over by military green. The once neat row of business casual church attire had been shoved over into the far back, crowded out by rows of stiff camo. Brown loafers were made to look diminutive in comparison to enormous combat boots. I wondered if I would be able to launder these new uniforms appropriately. The labels came with no instructions. None of this came with instructions.

I swaddled Lyla up tight in her white linen blanket with pink and purple birds flitting about in a pattern and lay her in her crib.

There's always a moment when bringing a new baby home when time hits pause. It hovers in place in an overall feeling of—
*Now what?*

Then, in a flash, the new baby lets you know with a squawk, a soiled diaper, or a bout of crying that has no cure and must be painstakingly waited out. It is this way with the Missing, too. At times, the Missing can become so violent, so intense, that the crying seems to have no end. There is no cure, no reprieve. You simply have no choice but to cry until the tears run out.

Just as I had colic with the Missing, Lyla had colic, too.

There should be a cosmic rule that if you have a baby during a season of great trauma or grief, the baby should be easy. By default, you should get the kind of baby that only cries when they're hungry or needs a diaper change. They should be predictable and sweet and easy to soothe.

Lyla was no such baby.

Oh, she was sweet. She was as sweet as they come, but she was far from easy.

When the sun went down, she would squirm and writhe in pain and cry. I held her tight in her swaddle. I bounced with her and shushed her. I passed her off to C.J. when I could and to my mom at other times, but even with them, I didn't feel like I could ask for their help. I was the mama after all. Lyla needed *me*.

I hurt. My body hurt. Breastfeeding pinched. My toes curled in agony every time Lyla latched on. I sought help. I went to all the experts. I went to the lactation clinic to try to solve the issues Lyla and I were facing. I asked three different doctors about it. But nobody had any real solutions.

So I continued to hold her to my inflamed, cracked breasts and allow her to latch on. As her crying stopped, mine would start. My toes curled and tears streamed every time Lyla would eat. Every two to three hours, I would go into the torture chamber that was the rocking chair in Lyla's pretty nursery. I was determined to be successful at breastfeeding and not make the same mistakes I felt I had made when Jude was an infant. I didn't want C.J. to feel the pressure of the expense of formula. *This is how God made my body*, I told myself. *This was the natural thing. If I kept at it, eventually it would click.*

And yet without fail, the sun would go down and the crying would start. Lyla would scream so hard she would turn a particular shade of reddish purple, which could have been a pretty nail polish color, but on a baby, it was absolute agony.

The Missing paced the nursery with me. Lyla would only partially quiet if I stood with her, held her on her side, and pressed her belly against my own. In that posture, I kept a gentle bounce.

It was our own march. Back and forth I rhythmically shushed her.

"Sh. Sh. Shhhh. Sh. Sh. Shhhh."

The Missing hissed with me, sitting on my shoulders while I clung to the swaddled bundle. With white knuckles, I clung. I clung to the baby, and I clung to my sanity—which was quickly slipping through my tired grasp.

One dark night, my arms felt too weak. Everything got too heavy. The tears burned my eyes. I couldn't breathe through the weight in my chest. I pictured myself simply dropping the baby to the floor. Liberating my arms from their burden. Nothing I was doing was working.

*If a baby falls in the nursery and no one is there to hear it...* no one but me. Broken, consumed by the Missing—me.

C.J. slept unaware in the other room, having given up hours ago. The Missing had ushered my mom into the basement where she would stay until morning.

No one was there to help me, and I would have to get used to this. This crushing independence. The full weight of responsibility. I felt unbelievably alone. Orphaned. Failing. Abandoned.

But I didn't drop her. Even with the Missing settling its full weight into my arms. I look back on this moment of pure weakness. Looking back, I know someone else was in that nursery with me—another set of arms holding me up instead of pushing me into the purple polka-dotted rug on which I was wearing my path.

I honestly don't know how I didn't just let her fall and stumble away into the night. Somehow, I kept holding her. I kept bouncing. I kept the military beat going in the colicky moonlight.

*Sh. Sh. Shhh. Sh. Sh. Shhh.*

*Abba, I belong to You.*

## THE FIRST FAREWELL

C.J. left exactly one month to the day after Lyla's birth. In the darkness of the early morning hours, my toes once again made fists while I nursed my infant in the hopes she would sleep the duration I was gone to drive C.J. to the airport and not wake my mom who was still in the basement.

Experience has since taught me that, in some ways, the looming of goodbye is worse than the goodbye itself. Much like the agony of waiting for an inevitable last breath, it is a torturous limbo to be caught in with the Missing poised to strike at any moment.

I was more than ready for this particular goodbye to be over with.

C.J. loaded his enormous green duffel bag into the trunk of our car. He drove. We held hands. I know his hands as well as I know my own. His gold replacement ring was in its rightful place on the fourth finger of his left hand. By all appearances it was identical. No one would know that it was no longer the original ring signifying the commitment made on our wedding day. In some ways, it was fitting. Our marriage was on the cusp of a new season—from this point on, the military would be a determining factor in the nature of our relationship. *It* would dictate where we would live and the time we would spend apart. Our freedom as a little family was ironically now far more limited than it had ever been.

It had been unbearable watching him tuck Jude into bed the night before. The thought of Jude asking where his Daddy was when he awoke weighed heavy. I dreaded facing that moment. He wasn't going to understand. There just isn't the language to adequately explain divine callings and a duty to country to a 3-year-old. All he would know was that his father tucked him into bed the night before and was gone in the morning.

He would awaken to a crying baby sister and an exhausted mother. Then the Missing would step in. The Missing would linger near my son, take him by the hand, and remind him who wasn't there.

I walked with C.J. into the airport. My body still felt the aftereffects of pregnancy. My hips were stiff, and my legs lacked strength. Again, the surrealness of the experience had me floating above myself. I watched the actress who looked like me kiss her husband and promise to write to him every day.

I thought maybe if I romanticized the experience, it would be more bearable. I envisioned myself as one of the World War II women who sent sailors off to war with their red lips and waving handkerchiefs. But he wasn't even in uniform and waving him off in his regular jeans and t-shirt kind of killed the fantasy.

No, there wasn't anything romantic about this. Every hole in my body was leaking—draining out. I felt empty.

Driving home, the sun was just beginning to rise. The song on the radio was Sarah Bareilles' "Brave." I belted the words, *"I want to see you be brave"* out between sobs. I didn't know who I was singing about—me or C.J.—but, either way, the anthem of being one's true self was exactly what I needed as I wailed.

I returned to a quiet home. I climbed back into my empty king-sized bed.

The Missing greeted me with its snide cheek on C.J.'s pillow. I rolled over onto my left side, turning my back to its vacant presence.

Exhausted but wide awake, I stared out my bedroom window. The ink-black night sky turned to navy blue and then gray, giving way to gold. Dawn broke. I waited for my children to rise with the sun. I waited for the peace that surpasses understanding that is promised in the Bible to settle in. It didn't. The closest thing to peace I felt in that moment was cold, empty, and numb. There was no space for brokenness. I willed myself not to give in to self-pity.

*Abba, I belong to You.*

## THE HOMEFRONT

I did write to C.J. every night.

I was angry with him for leaving us, but I kept the venom and vinegar out of my letters. Instead, they were full of the mundane. It was more of a daily account of what the kids and I were up to rather than a deep dive into how I was truly feeling. I was merely a secretary taking the minutes.

*Today we went for a walk. We saw some geese. Fall is coming.*

To heap my true emotions on him would be selfish, I reasoned. If I were to open Pandora's box of honesty and put that in the letters, the paper might burst into flames. I didn't want him to worry. I needed him to focus on what he was doing there. I tried not to think about the big changes that were ahead of us because of this decision. I kept my eyes on the path directly ahead of me and focused on caring for my two little ones. That was more than enough for now.

I rarely heard back from C.J. In Officer Candidate School, they are locked down tight as they undergo their rigid training. For each daily letter I sent, I got one back from him every two weeks or so. Yet every evening, I walked the 30 steps to the mailbox anyway to mail my letter. There's something about fresh air that removes the mask of pretense and honesty is revealed. The Missing came with me for my nightly ritual.

I missed C.J. I missed the security of his presence. I missed there being two parents for Jude and Lyla who could divide and conquer, instead of just me having to do it all. I missed who we had been in the past when our life was hectic but simple. I missed the butterflies of falling in love when we could go on date nights and flirt and laugh and he could hold me while I cried. Instead, my tears soaked the chest of the Missing.

I missed the days before the Missing moved in. I missed when I could talk to my dad in person rather than send tearful one-sided messages up to Heaven or when moonlight was just moonlight—when it was only beautiful and never sad.

I was just so tired of *missing*. Missing Dad. Missing C.J. Missing it all.

On my walk to the mailbox with the Missing as my companion, I reminded myself that as much as I missed C.J., at least *he* wasn't dead. He would be back. And as angry as I felt toward him in this moment, I knew that somehow we would stumble into this unknown future together.

---

*I longed for a reprieve. I craved sleep that seldom came.*

*Nightly, the Missing sat beside my bed and projected the most traumatic of my memories on the ceiling above my bed. From the uselessness of my pillow, I relived the worst of my mental reel again and again and again. The sound of dying. The smell of death. The violent taking. The empty warmth that would turn cold.*

*In my mind, I walked the halls of the funeral home. The hospital. The phone conversations that brought pain. The feeling of broken earth beneath my feet. The tearing away. The guilt that came with the relief of it being over.*

*Even the moon brought pain because it had dared to shine beautifully over the most heinous of nights. I resented its audacious constancy.*

*If sleep came, the Missing followed me into my dreams. It teased me with visions of what had been or could have been. The only thing real about the dreams were the tears on my cheeks when I finally awoke—punctuated with a painful jolt of fresh reality.*

## CHAPTER 7

# In Pursuit of the Missing

I traveled with C.J.'s mom and stepdad to his graduation from OCS in Alabama.

I can still hear Jude's high-pitched cry of joy when he saw his daddy in dress blues, complete with a strange, pointy hat, walk up to the hotel lobby where we were staying. Jude's legs were faster than the automatic sliding door, and he nearly ran splat into the glass in his efforts to get to his father's arms.

The purity of the moment hangs on the wall of my memory. This would be the first of many joyful yet battered reunions.

The rest of the short time we spent there is a collage of intense, sharp images. Much of it I spent clutching Lyla in my tired arms. Everything I'd packed to wear was covered in her spit-up.

I hadn't the slightest clue what to wear for the occasion. I'd chosen stretchy jeans and a loose top in an effort to minimize my maxed-out postpartum frame, noticeably more casual than was customary. I didn't speak this military language. I didn't understand the traditions. I was a fish out of water on the shore of a foreign land—eyes wide and gulping for air.

Still, I tried to smile proudly. I *was* proud. C.J. graduated with honors. He was chosen as the Distinguished Graduate of his class. His mom and I stood on either side of him to pin the Officer bars onto his uniform. He'd lost weight from all of the physical training he'd endured and quick meals he'd learned to scarf down in an allotted time frame.

That night, alone with the baby in my hotel room once again, waves of nausea overtook me. I found myself throwing up half the night. To this day, I'm not certain if it was food poisoning or an aversion to the life I had found myself thrust into. Whichever it was, I ended up crumpled on the hotel bathroom floor—dehydrated and empty.

My breasts no longer produced enough milk to feed my colicky infant. My stomach heaved dry. I had nothing left. It was as if large hands had taken me and wrung me out like a wet rag.

The Missing sat on the tile floor with me, quiet but present.

Perhaps you've found yourself on the floor. In moments of deep grief and pain, I've often responded by crumpling to the floor, knees buckling under the weight of the Missing. I've lain on my kitchen floor and wailed the siren of impending death. I've huddled in the corner of my closet, doing my best to keep my unraveled sobs hidden from my children.

My guess is many of us who grieve have found ourselves on the floor—flattened by the waves that break one right after the other. Yet somehow, we peel ourselves off of the sticky, apple juice and goldfish cracker crumb-laden surface. We wipe our faces with our sleeves and emerge from the dark closet. Somehow, we continue to function. We show up to work. We make our bed. We begin to accomplish the mundane because we know we must.

Somehow, we crawl from the bathroom floor and give to our helpless infant from the emptiness of the Missing.

*Abba, I belong to You.*

## THE UPROOTING

C.J. came home and I had my first experience with what is called "*reintegration*." It's that period of time when a family is reunited after having been apart for a significant season.

We were so glad to have OCS behind us, but now it was time to think about what was next. C.J. received orders to report to Florida to undergo his initial nine-month training for what his job would be. Rather than be apart for nine months, we decided we would uproot our family and move temporarily.

So, the day after Christmas, two men who looked like weathered 80s metal band members, complete with long frizzy mullets and acid-washed jackets, came to pack up our belongings. They blasted ZZ Top and wrapped my dishes in packing paper. We weren't going to be taking all of our things with us, but with the military paying for the movers, we did want to take enough that we could settle in comfortably for the length of our stay.

My mom had come to spend Christmas with us. The last Christmas where we'd gathered in her home with Dad felt like another lifetime. Now, she helped clean my house and get it ready for our temporary renter.

"Why do I feel like we won't be coming back?" I asked her.

"You may not." Mom is never one to mince words or withhold the truth of what she's thinking.

A few days later, we said what were supposed to be temporary goodbyes, loaded into our cars, and pointed them south. Lyla miraculously slept most of the two-day journey to Panama City, Florida. It was just me and her in my little red Jetta. I drove with my left hand and stretched my right arm into the back seat to hold the bottle for her.

The Missing rode shotgun.

Finally, we emerged from our cars and stiffly unfolded into the Florida air, which surprisingly smelled really bad. The unfamiliar stench wafting from the nearby paper mill assaulted my nostrils. My nose immediately scrunched into its accordion of wrinkles.

At 5 p.m., or 17:00 in the new language I would have to learn, the Star-Spangled Banner began to play over the loudspeakers filling the base with an instrumental of the anthem. C.J. immediately snapped to attention. I wrangled a spit-up-soaked Lyla out of her car seat to stand to my own version of attention, hoping a squalling infant baby wouldn't be seen as the height of disrespect. I scanned the area for a flag to look at. Not finding one, I set my eyes upward.

Up toward the sky, toward heaven. Searching for a window that maybe Dad could be looking through.

Rather than standing in stoic silence, the Missing waved its arms conducting the invisible orchestra.

I'm sure I was supposed to feel a swell of patriotism—a pride that comes with serving one's country. Instead, I felt panicked. It was eerie and uncomfortable. Nothing about that situation was familiar—except for the smell of spit-up.

The Missing spun around my golden son. Jude's cherubic face was alert and solemn. He dutifully placed his pudgy right hand over his heart. The sight caused mine to shatter into pieces all over again.

## BASE LIFE

We moved into base officer's housing, which was quite nice. Three bedrooms, and a decent amount of space—I quickly unpacked and made it ours. Home sweet home for the next nine months.

Though my family did its fair share of cross-continent road trips, I'd never been to Florida. The unique landscape of the Florida panhandle was a surprise to me. I expected palm trees and sunshine. Instead, the late December air was chilly, and rows upon rows of straight pine trunks with their prickly evergreen tops rushed by the car window resembling the brushes I used to wash Lyla's bottles.

To reach the entrance to the base, you drive over a beautiful, long bridge. Down below, ocean waters sparkled, and boats zipped by. I often had to remind myself to keep my eyes on the road in front of me rather than scanning the surface for the rainbow-shaped tops of dolphins arching up and down in the sparkling, crystal blue water.

The Florida panhandle is also infested with bears. Yes, bears. We were told to keep our garbage cans inside the garage and not bring them out until the morning of trash day. Bears were spotted often wandering the base housing. It felt strange giving Jude instructions to watch where he stepped for snakes and if he saw a bear, to immediately run to tell a grownup.

We quickly made friends. The many playgrounds on base and the nomadic lifestyle of military families means there is no time to waste. There was no shortage of friends for Jude, and exhausted, threadbare stay-at-home moms for me. Daily, we gathered at the playground or in our driveways.

This was my crash course in military life. Being the novice that I was, these women did their best to instruct me on the many acronyms that popped up in conversation and the way things are typically done in military culture. Some of them had been in the military for many years, so I lapped up their experience and tried to make sense of where I found myself.

Mostly I learned that military wives possess a depth of strength I hadn't ever seen before. They are like the twist ties that hold the bread bag closed—flexible, yet strong. Their lifestyle has conditioned them into being comfortable with the unknown.

I sat beside a woman whose husband had been in the service for years. Side by side, we sat on the blue playground bench the morning her husband left for a year-long deployment. Puffy eyes told the story. The Missing sat beside her. Her regal chin was set on brave, and, for the moment, she seemed to have the Missing completely tamed. It was as if she had told it to *"sit,"* and now an obedient pup, it complied and waited patiently for its cookie.

Oh, the bitterness was there too. The temper tantrums of children who missed their fathers were commonplace on the playground. These mamas, and at times dads, would scoop their child up and try to be two in one.

The Missing and I took it all in. One night, walking into the gym on base, the moon was bright and full in the sky above me. I heard Dad's voice as clear as if it was coming through the on base speakers that played the anthem.

"Did you ever think you would live in Florida?! Wow. God is good."

The sound stopped me in my tracks in that parking lot. The Missing heard it too and halted its shadowy gait alongside me. Moonlight bounced off the glistening asphalt, sparkling like a million diamonds.

I took a breath, breathing in the beauty of the moment. The familiarity of the voice. Then I kept walking, plodding forward. One foot in front of the other.


## RETURN TO HOME

The Missing gripped my shoulders and ushered me forcefully along the taped-off route leading to the Canadian customs agent in his glass booth. It fed me my lines into my ear; the answer

I had practiced in my mind to the question that I knew was coming.

*"Who are you coming to visit?"*

*"My mom,"* I would answer.

I reminded myself I no longer had two parents. The plural had become singular. The parental unit had been severed. What had been my parents' home was now occupied by only one.

I had to learn new habits with even my words. The first time hearing only my mom's voice on what had been *their* answering machine nearly shocked me into a mute stupor. My conditioned response had always started with, "Hey, guys…" Now, I must address only mom.

I answered the agent's questions and presented my passports and my notarized note of permission from C.J. to travel out of the country with our children.

I tried to push away the memory the Missing shoved in my face of the last time I'd approached the customs agent to answer the same questions. I had completely fallen apart when he asked me what my parents did in Winnipeg. I had blubbered that my Dad was dying and he wouldn't be *doing* anything anymore.

I'd never seen an agent stamp a passport so quickly.

We'd come all the way from Florida. Exhausted from three separate airplanes on my own wrangling two kids, I gladly relinquished bath time to my mom as soon as we walked through the red door.

This was my first time back since the funeral. The Missing pushed by me and spread its arms wide as if to say,

*"Honey, I'm home!"*

A photo of Dad, the one that we framed to sit atop his casket, was now displayed on the corner cabinet in the living room. There he sits. With a mischievous twinkle in his eye and a smile on his lips, it looked as though his gaze was fixed on his family in the room, observing and laughing, much as I pictured him doing from his window in Heaven.

The dining room we'd temporarily turned into the bedroom where Dad would spend the last months of his life now contained a portable crib for Lyla. Instead of medicine bottles and Kleenex and a walker, there were now baby bottles, diapers, and binkies.

Sitting down in Dad's leather chair by the window, the Missing weaseled its bony hip to sit with me in claustrophobic closeness. It leaned in with its suffocating lily breath and backhandedly reminded me Dad had never held this baby.

Looking out the large front window at the Narnia lamp post, I wondered how Mom was managing now it was lawn mowing season. Without my brothers and my dad to carry the load, it was all up to her now. Dad had always worked hard to keep the lawn green and filled in—forever moving the sprinkler around the yard to fill in the brown spots. Now it looked kept, but a bit patchy. The brown, dead spots—footprints of the Missing.

This was the first home my parents had ever owned outright together. All of their previous homes had been World Impact staff housing. With a stucco exterior and impossibly squeaky floors, Dad and Mom had settled in and made it theirs.

Dad wasted little time adding a bathroom in the basement. It was there I brushed my teeth after getting the kids to bed. I felt the cool tile beneath my feet. Tile laid by my dad's hands.

The Missing tingled with illumination. Every nail, every smell—it all pointed to Dad.

I pushed my way through the ugliness of the Missing's main course of memories to get to something sweeter—memories of that Christmas many years ago when I was 5 years old, coming down the stairs to a wooden dollhouse almost exactly my height. Yellow with white trim. A magical gift just for me built by my father. It came with a perfect, miniature family—a mother and a father.

A tiny plastic father immune to cancer. Incapable of aging. As alive as I wanted him to be because I was sovereign over that tiny universe. Nothing there happened without my permission. My hand initiated every change. Predictable. Controlled. Transcendent and ordinary all at once.

It was the last thing I saw before drifting off to sleep. The tiny plastic father immortalized in his tiny, plastic easy chair, reading a tiny plastic newspaper on which the date would stay tiny and plastic. Forever frozen in time.

## ROCK COLLECTING

I felt the sun on my back and the damp grass beneath me. We'd taken the day to drive the hour south to Dad's gravesite in Niverville.

Jude wandered around the granite tombstone, stooped to pick a dandelion, held it to his rosy lips, and sent wishes sailing through the air.

"I wish Grandpa Fred could come back," he said. If only dandelions held that power.

The ground in a graveyard always feels hollow to me. Hallowed. Hollow. Those words sound the same. I tend to tread lightly on the grass in a graveyard as if a hole could appear at any moment and swallow up my foot. When the ground has been dug up and displaced by caskets, I can't help but think that it feels softer, even with grass filled in over the top.

These were my deep thoughts as I walked between rows of stone.

In contrast to the early spring snow backdrop of our last visit, this time everything was green and canola yellow, butting up against the endless blue sky. These were the farmlands of my ancestors: the Mennonite communities that have toiled that land for generations.

Having long since left the lands of my upbringing and family, sometimes I imagine my roots with octopus legs skittering about the surface, searching earnestly for a place to dive. To find stability in the depths.

Yet here, the surnames on all of the tombstones were familiar. I could feel the vastness of my roots on these prairies. Roots that now dive and weave around this honeycomb earth. My own roots tingled at the thought.

Here on the Manitoba prairies, I had become more than a grieving daughter; I was a walking legacy. The descendant of the God-fearing and hardworking. As the chronically identity starved, this was a place of comfort rather than sharp pain.

I thought back to a time when Dad and I were driving together through these same Manitoba prairies, not far from this final resting place. As we drove, I hesitantly breached the subject of what his wishes would be should the cancer overtake him. We didn't talk often about the possibility of his death. Dad chose to live believing he would be healed and live a long life. His response went something along the lines of,

"I guess I would want a place where you, and whoever else wanted to, could remember me."

As if remembering him was contingent on location.

On this visit rather than try to keep the Missing at bay, I tried something different. Instead of fighting to tame it, I leaned into it. I stepped closer to it and rested my cheek on its shoulder. And with that gesture, I 'missed'. Oh, how I missed Dad. I allowed the full intensity of the Missing to whirl. He was worthy of great missing.

By that granite rock, I finally stopped fighting the Missing, and I set it loose.

The Missing rushed out in a swirling of prairie winds. I grabbed it by the tail and wrapped it around me, draping it around my shoulders and wearing it as my mantle.

My fingers gingerly touched the cracked earth. There, on that plot of sacred ground in the Manitoba prairies, I could sit all at once above and below him.

I thought, *Maybe if I reach, I can hold one of Jesus' hands and Dad can hold the other.*

A holy tether, hovering between—drawing heaven a little closer.

After a couple of minutes, I saw Jude reach down and pick up a rock from the gravel road that circled the graveyard. At first, I thought he was going to put it in his pocket to add to his rock collection he kept at home. Instead, he approached his Grandpa's headstone with a seriousness that aged him into a wise, old man and solemnly laid it on top.

I watched as he added a few more rocks, a scrap of fabric, and some dandelions—a small pile of offerings. I got the sense that he was trying to decorate the headstone, in an attempt to make it more beautiful. Perhaps believing that the stone itself was the source of my pain, he wanted to make it slightly more appealing for his mama.

It was also an unintentional and innocent nod to the Jewish tradition of leaving a rock on a grave as a marker you had been there. It reminded me too of the inukshuks in Canada and Alaska—piles of rocks arranged in formation which can be found beside roads, atop mountains, and randomly scattered throughout nature. Human-constructed rock structures that declare, *"Someone was here! This place is significant!"*

Even now, as I continue to walk through the challenging and ever-changing territory that is military life, I find I crave sacred spaces where the buildup of the Missing can finally be released from my shoulders and tumble away—as Christian's burden did down Calvary's hill in "Pilgrim's Progress."

Along this road of grieving, I find my soul collecting rocks. The Missing drops one in my hand at every birthday, holiday, or important event missed.

Each time Lyla's eyes flash that same color green that my dad's eyes held, the Missing reaches into its pocket and hands me a rock. When songs that were sung at his funeral come on the radio—plop, rock.

With every birth of a grandchild he will never hold, or a family gathering with an empty chair, or when I'm trying to remember how to start a lawn mower, another rock is added to my collection.

I find my hands are constantly full of rocks. I clumsily carry them and try to tune out their incessant whispering,

*Something significant happened here...*

I find I am relentlessly scouring the landscape for a place to lay them. Sometimes I can drop one or two pebbles. At church. In my journal. Staring across the ocean at the horizon. These are all altars on which I can lay some rocks.

But mostly I think about the large granite rock that sits on the prairie. The one that is held up by roots. There, I can let them tumble from my fingers in one big heap. There, it is easier to lean into the Missing as an embrace, rather than defending myself in a perpetual wrestling match.

There, with the rocks in my hands, I can build my altar and lay on it my sacrifice of dreams unrealized, longings unfulfilled. The things that should be but aren't. With open and empty palms, I offer up unanswered questions and weak praises.

And then I can walk away and leave them there.

All the while knowing my hands will soon be full of rocks again.

*Abba, I belong to You.*

---

*The Missing was a rude companion. Inserting itself into every conversation and social interaction. It was a whore for attention and demanded to be at the center, even as I sought normal friendships and relationships. If it caught me enjoying myself or laughing with too much ease, it aggressively intervened. It refused to be ignored or second-fiddled. With a flamboyant flourish, it drop-kicked any remnant of peace into the pit of anxiety. Any time I caught myself close to joy, it shoved my face into a pool of guilt, drowning it out of me.*

*Tired of the negativity, I decided to make the most of it. I tried to dress the Missing up with pretty words and songs of faith, but I soon felt foolish because it heckled me mercilessly in its ridiculous disguise. My songs lacked pitch. The words hovered in the air—meaningless and stale. The Missing refused to be my doll and shed its patchwork costume like the skin of a snake.*

## CHAPTER 8

# The Missing and the Search for Home

I was right.

We would not be moving back to Wichita.

There's always something exciting to me about the idea of pulling up stakes and moving to a new and different place. The side of me that is chronically adventure-starved loves the thought of selling everything and moving to a faraway country where I don't speak the language or understand the culture and I have to merge by immersion. It's all fun and games and internet searches, though, until the moving truck arrives, and, once again, you're saying your goodbyes and faced with the enormity of the change.

With the lure of available full-time positions, we decided to make the more permanent transition to central Georgia.

It wasn't a faraway, exotic country, but it felt as foreign to me as anything I'd encountered previously. It was a land of ant hills as big as Winnipeg snow drifts. Suddenly everywhere I turned it was, "yes ma'am." *Ma'am? When did I cross over that age threshold?* I soon learned that *"yes ma'am"* is as ingrained in the young Southern mind as *"yes please."*

In a torrential downpour, the enormous semi-truck pulled down our cul-de-sac cutting through the humidity like I imagine it would feel like to swim through Jell-O. It parked in front of the little rental home we'd found. It's all an exciting adrenaline rush of unpacking the dishes (again) and setting up your kids' beds (again) until the truck drives away, and you're left standing in a strange house in a strange land with the sound of two crying kids rising from somewhere beneath the mounds of beige packing paper.

Reality hit like a belly flop onto hard, flat water. The Missing took up a gargoyle perch atop the tall, rectangular prismatic wardrobe boxes and surveyed its new domain. It loves the unfamiliar. It loves discomfort and draws strength from the insecurity that comes with loneliness.

This humid air was hard to breathe. My body vibrated with the sting of the impact and began to unpack box after box, trying to figure out how we were going to put our life back together again.

The loneliness was unlike anything I'd ever felt before.

It was a foreign panic filling out Jude's school enrollment to have it dawn on me that I literally had nobody to write down as my emergency contact. *Could I write down the grocery store clerk, who had a kind smile and called me ma'am in a non-condescending tone?*

I left it blank.

## LEAVING LOS ANGELES

I'd moved a few times in my life before this move to the Deep South. My answer to the question, "Where are you from?" is complicated and long at best. Typically I respond, "Mostly Kansas." The truth is, I'm not certain of even that anymore.

My first move, and one of the most formative experiences of my childhood, was the year we took as a family on a sabbatical in Guatemala. My parents decided on this move against the advice of many of their co-missionaries and the World Impact leadership. One thing that I love and admire about my parents is they cared very little for the business side of things. They had only one boss—God Himself. Sometimes the decisions they made were contrary to what was considered practical.

They cared very little for promotions of status or pay. At one point Dad had been the director of the L.A. ministries, and, for one reason or another, he resigned from that position. It wasn't for him. Fundraising and corporate tie-wearing were not Dad's things. He stepped away from the desk and office to resume his regular rhythm, working eye-level with the people; the people he loved. The people with whom he found belonging. Mom says the World Impact leadership never treated Dad the same after that. I don't think they quite knew what to do with his rebel spirit.

He felt no urge to climb the corporate (even ministerial) ladder. He was more likely to move the ladder to a neighbor's house, then climb up and clean out their gutters.

Guatemalan friends knew how weary my parents were in the year following the L.A. Riots of 1992, and in the telling of stories from their homeland, planted the dream of taking us there. The summer before my fifth-grade year, the six of us loaded up into our Ford Aerostar minivan and drove away from all I'd ever known.

I remember looking back. I always look back. I can still see the picture in my mind. All I'd ever known to be home, the setting of my childhood, was now a mental snapshot from the back window of our moving car.

We drove away from the beige, boxy exterior and chain-link moat of protection. We drove away from the lemon and orange trees in the backyard, the playhouse Dad had built for me, the tire swing with brick pavers beneath, and the pink rose and geranium strewn flowerbed. We drove away from the enormous palm tree in the front yard I'd stood under and prayed a child's prayer asking Jesus into my heart. I can still feel the natural fingerhold on its trunk that I had gripped and attempted to climb under my right fingertips.

And that day, at the end of something and the beginning of another thing, we drove away from all of it.

## CROSS BORDER JOURNEY

Before we pointed the van south toward our final destination in Guatemala, we took the longest detour imaginable. We drove to Kansas to visit Mom's family, then up to Canada to visit Dad's. There, we picked up a small wooden trailer my grandpa built for us and packed for our year south of two borders (three, if you count Canada).

Finally, we found ourselves in Brownsville, Texas, awaiting approval to journey through Mexico. I don't think the border people knew what to think of us. We stayed in a cheap motel for a week before we were finally allowed to travel to the shiny silver fence that identified the border. We waited all day in the long line. Still, they did not let us through. The sun went down, and they herded all those in line to within the silvery fenced area between the U.S. and Mexico to 'sleep'. In between two worlds we waited. And waited.

It was late summer and hellaciously hot. The mosquitos were ravenous for my pale, white skin. When the news speaks about the children in cages at the Mexican/ U.S. border, I picture the tall chain link fences that surrounded us on that hot, mosquito-filled night. I still feel that night on my skin.

None of us slept well. Dad set up a tent on the concrete ground. I opted to try to sleep in the van. It felt more secure than the thin vinyl tent.

In the morning, the officials finally let us through. They set us up with a caravan we were supposed to follow through Mexico—and we tried. Over the miles of pothole-ridden roads, we drove south until we finally reached the Mexico/ Guatemala border.

Approaching another border crossing, the anxiety rose in me. I was afraid. *Would they make us sleep in the tall chain-link cage again?* Fortunately, this border was much easier to get through, and the bribes did their work.

Soon our minivan and small wooden trailer were climbing up into the clouds. We pulled up to a bright turquoise adobe house that we could call home. It was on the property of a place called *Campamento Shalom.* It was run by Methodist missionaries on one side, and there was a Bible school run by the Presbyterians on the other. There were apple trees in our yard. We could pick apples directly off the tree and eat them.

Scattered in the hills behind our spot of turquoise were other small homes, dabbled between mountainside cornfields, identified by their puffs of smoke and laundry washlines. The Los Angeles skyline I could see from my bedroom window was replaced by twin volcanoes that rose into the sky in the distance: The Santa Maria and the Santiaguito.

From the playground at our private English-speaking school, we could watch when the Santiaguito sent puffs of ash into the sky. Dad and my older brother Aaron hiked to the summit of the Santa Maria. They carried along a mirror with which they sent a reflection down in the direction of our turquoise adobe home.

Standing in our front yard, I watched for the flash of light that signaled connection. The flashes came. We squealed in excitement, and I did my best to signal back with my own mirror.

I recall the relief I felt in that moment that Dad and Aaron were okay. They were making their way up into the clouds to stand on top of the world. With my two feet on solid ground down below, I envied their view but was also grateful I didn't have to do all that climbing.

## FAKING IT

Now, standing in the land of fire ants and enormous bows, I wondered, *Could Dad see me now?* I scanned the heavens for flashes of light signaling connection. Instead, he felt further away. The passage of time brought with it a new grief as the freshness of his presence and memories with him faded into soft focus. My feet sank with each step on the soft, rootless ground.

This was not a foreign country. In fact, I'd never seen more patriotic bumper stickers in my life. The language was the same—mostly. At times, I had to listen to some of the southern drawls with the same level of concentration I used when I lived with three roommates from Eastern Asia in college for a brief period in order to decipher what was being said. Their accents were so thick that despite focusing intently, sometimes I still nodded and faked understanding. They were sweet and patient with me.

It's a terrible thing to fake understanding, isn't it? To not feel the freedom to ask questions or ask for clarity as many times as you need to in order to actually understand. I'm afraid I'm guilty of faking understanding a lot in life. I don't want people to perceive me as ignorant or unintelligent.

I suppose this became a season where I faked understanding.

"God is God, and I am not," I would say. I understood that I was not Him, and therefore, I needed to trust that He knew what He was doing when He allowed the Missing to take the place of my dad.

"In this world you will have troubles," I recited. Of course, we're going to have troubles. I understood that. I chalked up

Dad's death as simply one of this world's sorrows. I stifled the questions the Missing kept flinging in my direction with platitudes and knocked them out of the air with reflexive Bible-quoting. I melded with the circumstances. I decidedly and intentionally skipped to the *'acceptance'* stage of the grief process. But truthfully, I wasn't even close.


## CHAMELEON SKIN

I've always prided myself on my ability to merge or blend in with cultures that aren't my own. It probably came from spending the majority of my childhood as the only white child in the room except for my siblings. I knew I was different. I figured it out eventually. I think it was the music that finally clued me in that I wasn't Latina like the majority of my friends.

While my friends' parents blared mariachi music and Selena, my parents demurely played Sandy Patti, Keith Green, and Mennonite choral music. A youth of the 70s, Dad also sang a line or two here and there from The Doors, The Beatles, Cat Stevens, and others. Their love of music was obvious, but the music they loved also made the difference between us and the community in which we lived obvious.

In Guatemala, my parents hired a Spanish tutor to teach us the language. I caught on quickly and was especially proud of my pronunciation. I wanted people to second guess identifying me as white. My goal was always to blend in as much as possible—to merge with those around me. I was forever standing out, and on many levels, although I was used to it, it was exhausting. My family was consistently pale and *'gringo'* against a backdrop of vibrant culture. I never knew anything different, and yet all I wanted—as most children do—was to fit in.

I vividly remember a time my older brother Aaron and I went to a roller rink with a teacher of ours. We were the only

White kids in the entirely Black crowd. It wasn't as if this was a new experience for me, but this time, we were on wheels. I was all too aware that not only did my pale skin stand out, but I couldn't skate. The smooth surface of a roller rink is very different from the ice of a bumpy Canadian pond! I was a timid white girl, who, like a gangly baby deer, was struggling to stay upright in a room full of amazing deeply melanated skaters. Everywhere I looked, a cool Black kid who knew the words to all the songs was flipping around to skate backward and doing the graceful skate-over-skate crossover turn at the curves.

Our friend had taken us there with the sole intention to have fun; instead, standing out was too much for me. I was *too* visible. When the DJ had everyone line up in two lines to do a Soul Train line and showcase their moves down the middle, I fell apart. I couldn't have any more eyes on me. I fled out the door and away from the crowds to take off my skates, leaving my brother and our teacher to wonder where I'd gone.

Blending in with my surroundings has become a driving force for me. I want to blend in just enough to not be weird but stand out enough to be special. I was quite proficient at it most of my life. With every move I made as a young adult, I merged with my surroundings. At college in Canada, I became just Canadian/ Mennonite *enough*. Marrying C.J. and joining the ministry at a large megachurch, I blended in. I spoke 'Christianese' fluently and had personal experience in every church duty that was deemed acceptable for an evangelical white woman.

With every mission trip I went on, I fell in love with the culture and made friends easily in those circumstances. Don't get me wrong, this wasn't fake. I wasn't faking who I was. It is one hundred percent authentic that I am a chameleon and capable of blending in with my surroundings and adapting to my environment enough to be accepted. I can relate to just about everyone. My chameleon skin is well-practiced.

Or at least this was the case until the Missing peeled it off of me. My chameleon skin didn't work like it once did. I was emotionally raw, and as much as I could fake understanding to stifle the questions that naturally spilled out of me, I couldn't fake *fine* very well or for very long. Merging with another culture or another place takes a lot of emotional energy, and I simply didn't have any to spare.

## FAR FROM HOME

I expected moving to Middle Georgia to be similar to the other moves I'd made in my life thus far. I would merge with the people and culture and make friends as quickly as I ever have.

"I can live anywhere," I told C.J.

Adapting to Warner Robins, Georgia, took a little more effort than I'd anticipated. It was harder than I figured it would be. I thought it would be relatively easy, seeing as it is not a foreign country, and visually I fit in just fine. Not only was the accent surprisingly difficult for me to understand, but the southern culture was different than anything I'd ever experienced. One of the things that struck me was the number of enormous bows on little girls' heads. I was quickly told, "The bigger the bow, the better the mother." I shamefully glanced at Lyla's fuzzy curls that hadn't been combed in a week.

There's a church on every corner here. First Baptist, Second Baptist, Sunnyside Baptist—you name it, there's a Baptist church with those words on the side of the building, and this is before we even touch the Presbyterians and various Assemblies that assemble.

I was ready to get back to church. Or so I thought. We hadn't attended regularly for almost a year at this point. Living on base in Florida had not been conducive to churchgoing. It was a long drive to get much of anywhere and with Lyla being so young, C.J. being swamped with homework, and the fact that the Missing was especially aggressive in a church setting—we simply didn't go. The few times I'd actually gone to church since Dad died had been difficult for me to get through. The grief hit hard. The Missing ran down my cheeks as I still wasn't able to sing without hearing his familiar baritone belting along.

You see, besides his wife and family, and Jesus, the church was Dad's other greatest love.

Now, living in the land of *church-on-every-corner,* I was ready to put that rhythm back in place for our family. I was ready to find our footing. If for anything, to have an answer to the constant follow-up question right after the "Pleased to meet you"—

"Have you found a church?" Church attendance is simply expected here.

Church felt like the closest thing to roots. It felt like the closest thing to the familiar. If I had a comfort zone, the church would be it. I felt like it should be easy to find a church here, but it ended up being more difficult than I could have expected.

We'd lived in the Bible Belt in Kansas, but this was a different sort of belt. This one was monogrammed and had a giant buckle embellished with a Confederate flag. I'd never been to the Deep South. And it was hard for me not to envision Harriet Tubman in the trees and landscape that blew past my car window even though her life never brought her this far south. Very few slaves escaped slavery in Georgia.

Any understanding or knowledge I had of the American South came from television, movies, and my school textbooks. I had a hard time separating what I was currently experiencing from the historical reputation the South has.

This land was more foreign to me than anywhere I'd ever been. Its customs and culture were difficult for me to comprehend, and understanding did not come easily. In fact, any standing I did during this season felt shaky. With my raw chameleon skin not functioning as it once did with the Missing's constant scraping, I struggled to feel any sort of belonging. My interactions felt forced.

The people we encountered were kind. Many were warm and welcoming to our little family who was devoid of any kind of support system. We were the recipients of the famous 'southern hospitality' time and time again. When you pair that with the camaraderie of the nomadic military community, we very quickly had a great number of people we could call on for help. This doesn't mean I did. It is a difficult thing to ask for help. To admit weakness. To show my vulnerable and insufficient side.

The Missing whispered in my ear, *"You don't need anyone. You have me."*

## A RARE AND IMPORTANT SERMON

The cotton fields were in full bloom when we arrived in Georgia. Their fluffy popcorn poufs bring the clouds down to meet the earth. My eyes, used to the wavy wheat of Kansas and the golden Canola fields of Manitoba, met the beauty of the cotton fields with a side eye and a sick feeling. My upbringing included a hefty dose of remembering the sins of our nation's past. I instinctively thought of the brown hands of the past that were forced to pick this fluffy, prickly white crop. I was shocked and appalled to find out it is common for white families to use cotton fields as the setting for their family portraits. I understood the aesthetic appeal, the fields are beautiful to look at— *'Georgia snow'* as it's called. Still, it seems calloused.

As a child, I sat in the congregation of church after church while Dad preached the same sermon time and time again. Piled in our minivan we toured through the areas of many of the churches that provided financial support to World Impact and, subsequently, my parents. Sunday after Sunday we walked into predominantly white congregations. I would sit in the long-upholstered pews, pulling my dress down as far as I could to provide a barrier between my skin and the scratchy fabric.

In a sea of white faces, still we stood out, and oftentimes we were asked to stand up when the pastor would introduce our family and welcome us to the church. This always embarrassed me. Mom and Dad sang too loud. They clapped when no one else was clapping. White churches don't really clap, at least not the ones we found ourselves in. We always had to sit toward the front so Dad could get to the pulpit easily. I could feel the eyes on the back of my head, and most of the praying I did was praying my ears weren't red.

The final note of the final song would vibrate in the silent room full of non-clappers. Then, Dad would walk up the carpeted stairs to the pulpit. The thick carpet muffled any steps, adding to the deafening quiet, so the final note hung in the air for what felt like an eternity until Dad finally got to his designated spot. There, he greeted the polite, expectant faces with a smile scanning the entire sanctuary from one side to the other as if attempting to make eye contact with every person there.

"Birds of a feather flock together, is how the saying goes…" And thus Dad launched into an entire sermon speaking out against racism. In this dynamic sermon, he emphasized the importance of repentance and pleaded for white congregations to engage in steps toward racial reconciliation. My back would stiffen in response—both out of pride and out of defensiveness.

Again and again, I listened to this sermon. Preached to sea after sea of pale faces. He took this sermon all across the Midwest and up to Canada. At least a dozen times, I heard that introductory phrase: "Birds of a feather flock together…"

I didn't realize how profoundly unique it was for a white pastor to tackle this topic until I was grown; until I realized White people as a general rule, tend to avoid the subject.

Now, I found myself in the Deep South: ground zero of American slavery and the hub of Jim Crow. My roots tingled on this blood-red Georgia clay. The echoes of my dad's sermon have stuck in my soul, and I find myself impassioned by the same things that spilled out of Dad from that pulpit.

Sure, my dad was a missionary and a preacher. He was a godly man who loved people and loved his Savior, but he was also a rebel. His was a feral Christianity—untamed and unboxed. Free. Without legalistic chains and manmade lines of division. In his journal, he declared his job title to be *"servant to all."*

Borders are meant to be crossed. Borders between countries and nations. Invisible, social borders between people. Borders put up by systems and color and class. All of these borders are meant to be stepped through and over and broken down if necessary.

I cannot adequately grieve my dad without grieving the things that grieved him: racism, man-made division, wolves in sheep's clothing, things done in the name of Christ that are actually anti-Christ—these are the things Dad spent his life being counter to. These are the things to which the Missing has made me hyper-sensitive, and I am determined to embody the legacy of my dad and the Jesus he loved. The Jesus who crossed borders too.

In many ways, coming to middle Georgia, where the shades of skin tones on the color wheel are vast and varied, was incredibly refreshing. Growing up surrounded by color and culture, entering a community where it was easy to cross racial lines felt like a balm to my soul. I was Fred's daughter after all. I had been raised by a man who left home as a young man with the sole intention of crossing socio-economic and racial lines. Part of me is still most comfortable and joyful in a room where I am the minority.

## THE PEACH STATE

Dad had only set foot on this red clay ground once in his lifetime. He'd flown to Georgia for my brother Aaron's graduation at the start of his Army career. By Dad's own admission, he wept over the young cadets as they marched in uniform, his firstborn being one of them. It's comforting to me that Dad had been to the state I now call home, though I wasn't with him at the time. He'd felt the sticky humid air, took in the towering magnolia trees, and listened to words cradled in a drawl.

Yet, the enormous semi commissioned by the military with our belongings was a far cry from my family's minivan with its small handmade wooden trailer.

In our new home, I stood lookout in the front yard with Jude and Lyla hoping to meet some friends. It was a different vibe than the nine months we'd just spent surrounded by playgrounds and ready playmates on base in Florida. Now, there was just silence. And bugs. And enormous ant hills that you wouldn't realize you'd put your foot in until the fire stabbings would begin, and you were left hopping, swiping the fire off with your flailing hands.

I spent most of my time rescuing Lyla, who'd just learned to walk, from toddling, arms stretched upward for balance, into the street. There were very few nearby parks to gather in.

C.J. began work immediately.

I began pouring myself a drink every night.

Dad rarely drank. I had a glass of wine once with Dad which led to an epically hilarious game of Pictionary in which C.J. sketched *"in the looking glass"* to which Dad guessed, "pig face!" Tears bounced down our faces in peals of laughter. That was the one and only time I'd seen Dad buzzed by a drink.

Now, I was alone. I couldn't even call Mom during those days because she was on her own journey traveling Asia and re-tracing our familial steps in Guatemala. She was busy climbing the Santa Maria at night with strangers helping her to the top so she could watch the sunrise from the summit. That's a book for another day.

C.J. was busier than ever and was sent away soon after our move for further training. Once again, it was just me and my children. I was alone with my energetic son and my toddling daughter, whose eyes mercifully and heartbreakingly had turned the same shade of green as Dad's. I was alone with the overwhelming newness of a world I no longer fit into.

The Missing and I sat on my porch. It grazed its fingernail on the inside of my forearm and traced the word 'home'. *Where was home?* The concept of home had shifted into a nebulous, abstract concept long before this move. Many will say, *"Home is a person"* but in a military family, I've learned this cannot be the case for us.

*Home is where the...*fickle heart is. And my heart can be the most fickle. Especially in grief. We must learn how to carry *home* within ourselves. Someone once said, losing a parent is like wanting to go home but you can't. This has been my experience.

When the sun would set and the kids were finally asleep, I would pour myself a hard drink and wait for the muscles in my jaw to unclench. A few sips in, I would anticipate my shoulders to feel the kind of weight that pushes them softly into the cushion instead of feeling the need to carry the heaviness. I didn't drink a large amount, but I drank with consistency every evening—just enough to push the Missing into the corner so I didn't have to think about it for even a little while.

I just wanted it to be smaller. I just wanted it to feel a little lighter. To be quieter and stop roaring in my ears. I couldn't seem to *'fake understanding'* with this middle Georgia world with its racist history, strange customs, and lack of playgrounds. With the Missing constantly pointing out how badly I fit in here and bringing up deep theological and systemic questions that I had no answers for, I wanted my dad.

But in the morning when I woke up, it was still there. There on its perch in the corner, up with the kids and the sun and the demand for peanut butter toast and annoyingly peppy cartoons.

What would Dad think to see his daughter turning to the source of so many of his friends' devastation as a coping mechanism to stop feeling the gaping Missing *he* left behind? A shot of guilt went into every drink I made for myself, and still I drank it down.

When a mouse invaded our house, the anxiety sent me spiraling into a stressed-out depression. I don't *do* mice. When we first moved into our World Impact staff house in Wichita, we caught over 40 mice. That is probably where my phobia stems from.

So, along with my nightly rum and ginger ale, I began to scan the ads for a new home. I needed to get out of that mouse house. I needed away from the loneliness and isolation I felt there. I needed out of nomadic limbo. I needed to feel some sort of consistency, some sort of security. I was desperate for *home*. I wanted to push roots down into the red, Georgia clay if for no other reason than to feel like I wasn't going to blow over in the storm clouds that continued to swirl around me.

C.J. made it home from SEER training and was able to slip into a full-time technician job on base. With this transition, our move to Warner Robins began to feel more permanent. Finding a house and getting out of the mouse-infested rental became an obsession.

The Missing massaged my tense shoulders in a rough, annoying way that, rather than relieving tension, caused it to spin up. The reality of living in Warner Robins permanently began to settle in. I would have to find a way to merge. To adapt. To engage with the strange culture and customs—and even embrace it. I would have to figure out how to forge friendships and learn from the relationships I was building. To look back at the past and apply it to my future. I would have to stop pouring myself drinks every night and stop numbing the Missing, which was also a permanent fixture.

We finally found our home where we currently live. With every load I hauled in the back of my minivan, I moved further away from the loneliness of the rental. I inched my way out of drunken limbo and noticed my skin already felt less raw.

Again and again, I pulled into the driveway of our new brick home with a spacious yard, chain link fence, and room to breathe. With every trip I took between the houses, I felt closer to establishing roots. I crossed over the threshold of what could be home, even as the Missing rode shotgun with a box in its lap.

I could leave the ferocious rodents behind, but I could not evade the Missing.

---

*I tried locking it in a room. Against the door, I built a barricade. I piled it high with distractions and to-do lists. Maybe if I worked hard enough and fast enough, I could keep the Missing locked away. Work harder. Pile higher.*

*To the pile, I added vices. Perhaps if I drank myself into a light-headed fog, I could pretend it wasn't there. Maybe I could stay in the blissful, numb place where I didn't have to feel, think, or function. My efforts always proved futile. The Missing always broke through. The fog would wear off, and the barriers crumbled with me in a heap of exhausted trying.*

*The Missing stepped over the rubble with a cruel grin that said, "nice try."*

*It reached for my wrists, its spidery fingers matching the crescent nail marks angry with chronic reopening. It put its face close to mine and with its lily breath hissed,*

*"Remember!"*

*At times I didn't know where I ended and the Missing began. We were an unholy merge. A possession for which there was no exorcism. Every day I felt its violence. Every day I waited for spiritual and emotional annihilation. Every night I went to sleep with the Missing, and every morning I woke up to the Missing.*

## CHAPTER 9

# The Missing Grandpa

Shortly before Dad died, I had a dream. In this dream, I was dragging Jude by the arm and rushing along. I was desperate to get to Dad so he could bless Jude before he passed away—Old Testament style. I wanted Dad to put his hands on Jude's head, slather him in oil, and say the words found in Numbers 6. Words I'd heard Dad say hundreds of times from the front of the church at the conclusion of each service:

*"The LORD bless you and keep you; the LORD make his face shine on you and be gracious to you; the LORD turn his face toward you and give you peace."* (Numbers 6: 24-26 NIV)

I awoke before I could get to Dad, with tears on my cheeks and a catch in my throat. By this point, in real life, Dad's mind and voice were too far gone for him to recite a blessing over his grandson.

After Dad's passing, my grandpa, Dad's dad—instinctively laid his hands on Jude and Lyla's heads and breathed this holy benediction down their necks. His voice was quiet and raspy—the Missing was moving in on him too through Parkinson's disease—but the pastoral rise and fall of his cadence was still there.

I found I couldn't even hold my head up at that moment and leaned onto Grandpa's shoulder and wept. The Missing rushed around me in a swirl of emotion I was powerless to control. I didn't even have to ask. Somehow Grandpa knew. In place of his son, he spoke the blessing over my children. The moment was thick with the profound and supernatural. I could feel the branches in my family tree bending to embrace me in its protection. I could feel the generations past collide with the generations of the future—anointed in blessing and identity and eternal love. I could feel Dad. I could feel his hands in the midst. I could feel his familiar hand outstretched from Heaven, like God to Adam in Michelangelo's Sistine Chapel painting.

They were so alike, Dad and Grandpa. Both mustached. Both pastors. Both always ready to speak words from the Bible and talk about the One it's all about.

These words of blessing over my kids were the last I would hear Grandpa say. He joined Dad in Heaven just months later. No doubt they had much to discuss, as they often did around Grandma's lace-adorned dining table when they were together in this life.

Now they are both replaced by the Missing. They are stories and memories and legacies. I sit in the shade of their branches and watch my children play. Their heads glisten with holy oil, golden in the sunlight. Together we sit and ponder blessing and legacy and roots. Me and the Missing.

## IF ONLY

"Do you know who that is?" I pointed at a photo of Dad smiling enormously with Jude perched high on his shoulders.

"No," my son replied. The one-syllable word delivered a sharp stab to the heart.

"That's your Grandpa Fred." I pushed the words around the Missing which had lodged itself in my throat.

That's the problem with kids—they grow up. As they grow, the memories they have fade into the basement of their formative years. Jude was the only child to have formed any kind of relationship with my dad. To have been held by him. To have interacted and played with him. At one time Jude *knew* his Grandpa Fred.

He was the only grandchild to have Christmas with Dad. On Jude's first Christmas, he received a homemade Christmas ornament from him—a tiny but all too real screwdriver hanging on a silver ribbon. On the butt of its handle, Dad had penned in his familiar handwriting: *For Jude, Real tool #1 Love, Grandpa.* He'd even taken the time to wrap black electrical tape around the metal Phillips head to protect baby Jude's gums as he would undoubtedly use them to explore the tool like he did with anything else he got in his pudgy grasp during those drooly days.

Dad wasn't a gruff or disinterested grandpa. He was the type of grandpa that hip-checked me aside to push the stroller. He was a get-on-the-ground type of grandpa. In just about every photo I have of him with Jude, he is laid out flat on his stomach, eye-to-eye with his grandson. In one photo, he even has his head wedged underneath Jude's baby play gym, anything to get closer. To be nose-to-nose and face-to-face.

Seven of Dad's grandchildren currently walk this earth. He got to hold Jude, and he talked to Lyla in utero, but that was the extent of his grandpa career. There are times I can't help but spit with piss and vinegar, *"What a waste."*

Sometimes I hold my loss up against other people's losses. *Would I rather Dad had died suddenly? That instead of the gradual 9-year-long fade, he was just—gone?*

Sometimes I attempt to reason with the Missing that it's not as big a deal as it may think. I argue that it really is perfectly normal for a person to lose their parents. It is the natural progression of life. I would have eventually buried Dad regardless, even if he had lived to be 100. *And if he'd lived a long life, would it really have been any easier to say goodbye to him?* I suppose, in many ways, along with grieving the man himself, I'm mostly grieving the countless little moments he was *supposed* to still be here for.

I grieve the holidays without him. The weddings. The graduations. The first steps taken without his cheering. The sound of my children calling him Grandpa. The birthday cards without his handwriting. I grieve for the Christmas ornaments that should have been given to my other two children.

I try to shrink the Missing and make it smaller than it is. I haven't lost a spouse. I was a grown adult by the time Dad died, and there is gratitude in that. Those who have lost loved ones by violence or suicide—my guess is their Missing is a much more ferocious monster.

I've heard it said that *"loss is loss."* Whether it is the loss of a loved one, a marriage, a job, a beloved pet, or a house. All of these are painful and are owed their own grief. But I still think perspective is a powerful antidote against bitterness. For example, when I hear of someone losing a child, my empathy cannot extend so far. I cannot fathom such a loss.

Still, my loss was great. Every time I watch a grandpa at the park open a snack for his grandchild, I am back in the hospital reaching for a still-warm hand that would ultimately turn cold. It's in those moments I think, *"What a waste."* What a waste of a good grandpa. It makes it all worse knowing that Dad would have been one of the best grandpas. I can so easily picture it: Dad, in his typical white, New Balance tennis shoes (as many older gentlemen wear, I can't help but notice) chasing his grandkids around, laughing— and inventing games. I can see him filling up water bottles and pulling crust off sandwiches to feed to the birds. I see his purposeful gait as he walks a stinky diaper to the garbage for me—all of the mundane tasks that go along with being around kids. What makes it even more painful is the ease with which I can envision it. The Missing whispers *'If only'* in my ear.

*'If only'* he could have lived just a few more years.

*'If only'* he could have been here for the wedding, the graduation, the baptism, the firsts and lasts of life. It felt wrong to attend my grandpa's funeral without my dad there. It just isn't the proper order of things.

Having him around just a little longer sounds wonderful. There would be more memories to carry us through.

I have since realized there is a small blessing in Dad dying when Jude was yet small and unaware. I have learned it is a special kind of pain to watch your kids experience the ruthlessness of grief and not be able to do anything about it. I've had to watch them grapple with having a dad at home one day, and then finding him gone the next—whisked away on deployment or for training. I've seen the Missing as the puppeteer, influencing their behavior and stoking their anxiety while they learn to live with big feelings and bigger missings.

I've held Lyla as she wailed and threw fists at me when I had to tell her Uncle Kip, C.J's uncle who lived near us for a year and with whom she had a special bond, had passed away. I watched silent tears stream down Jude's face while I explained to him my mother-in-law had been diagnosed with ALS, a disease for which there is no cure. Together, C.J. and I and our children had a front row seat to a new Missing that came in as an evil witch, to gradually turn this vibrant and involved fixture in our world to stone. It was as if our souls were paralyzed along with her body. It is a new level of helplessness to watch my children be forced into grief, especially when I still feel so ill-equipped in my own.

*How do I teach them to grieve when I don't fully understand it myself?* I want to keep the Missing far away from my babies, but it is not up to me. I have often found the Missing snuggled up beside them on their beds during tearful pillow ruminations, to which I helplessly stroke their hair and whisper weak prayers. I cannot protect them from this pain, I can only join them in it.

At times I feel cheated that my grandparents weren't around the majority of my childhood either because of distance and death. Now, my children have since been cheated out of two grandparents: my Dad and my mother-in-law.

The robbery continues.

## A LONG WALK

Sometimes I envision a nursery in Heaven, where the babies wait for their turn to be sent to their designated womb. I'm not at all convinced of the theology of this, but I like to picture Dad hanging out with his grandkids before they were even an embryo. Maybe it happens in that window of time during an expectant mother's cycle, where she is pregnant but it's still too early to take a test. She is fully pregnant yet fully unaware. Only God knows. And I like to think maybe Dad did too, at least when it came to his grandkids. Perhaps he even got the inside scoop on a birth announcement.

I envision him in that heavenly nursery holding the hand of the grandkids that never lived outside the womb. The ones who are equally precious to the ones separated from him by a celestial veil.

Sometimes I wonder if he put in a personal request when he got to heaven that Lyla's eyes would be green like his. Of course, Jesus would grant his request. They are old friends, after all. Though the bitter side of me questions where this friend was when Dad was begging from beneath his damp washcloth,

"I want to live, I want to live, I want to live."

When I found out I was expecting my third child, I wept. The Missing gawked at the pregnancy test with me. I envisioned Dad leaning over the arm of Jesus' throne sitting next to Him as old friends do when they make smart-ass comments in the back of the room during important meetings.

*"Should I give them another one?"* Jesus asks.

*"Of course!"* Dad responds in laughter. *Of course.*

C.J. was gone for the majority of my third pregnancy. When he deployed in February, we were again uncertain if he would even be home in time for the birth in May. The Missing and I sat on the porch swing and rocked slowly, watching Jude and Lyla play in the front yard. My ankles were as swollen as my belly. Time seemed to stand still—caught up in the slow, ruminating creak of the porch swing.

We took tedious, waddling walks to the mailbox, checking for letters from overseas. Handwritten letters addressed to Jude and Lyla from their daddy written in his familiar handwriting— something to ease the harsh missing.

The Missing drew me back to the memory of Dad coming to visit me in Wichita when I was in my final weeks of pregnancy with Jude. I was enormous but trying to stay active. Dad and I went for a walk. It was late spring, and the lilacs were blooming. Going for a walk with Dad is something I did frequently with him when we were together.

Dad liked to walk. His white tennis shoes walked many miles of the city streets in which he lived. Dad was a big believer in walking the neighborhood. He said hi to everyone who crossed his path. He knew the old ladies sitting on their porches and could often be found sitting with them. When we planted United at the Cross Community Church on the south side of Wichita, Dad knew the streets, the homes surrounding the church building, and their inhabitants like the back of his hand. Many of our church regulars from those days could trace back their initial connection to Dad knocking on their door.

In Winnipeg, he did the same thing. He walked, befriending the homeless and meeting as many people as possible.

When the cancer broke both of his hips and he could no longer walk without pain, he began to volunteer for Meals on Wheels. That way, he could drive to the loneliest of people and bring them food. When he had his grand mal seizure and his license was taken from him, Mom obligingly drove him. Even when he was forced to use crutches or a walker, he walked. Feet to pavement or sidewalk, he refused to give up on his calling of being *a "servant to all."*

The month before he died, he was so pleased with himself because he'd walked to the grocery store two blocks away from their house and bought Mom flowers and a card for her birthday. I could hear the joy that came from reclaiming his independence in his broken words on our Thursday phone call. He'd gone all by himself.

Unbeknownst to us, his walking days would soon be coming to an end, so it was fitting that his last errand was on behalf of his favorite person on this planet—Mom.

The day we went for a walk under the lilacs with Jude's large head sitting heavy in my pelvis and my ankles swelling with each step, Dad scolded me for wearing cheap flip-flops. We ended up walking a bit too far from my house, and I almost didn't make it home. Dad's eyes were concerned. I could see his brain working trying to determine whether or not to take his cue from his independent and stubborn, but very pregnant daughter. He gently offered to leave me there and come back for me in the car.

I was both his daughter and now almost a mother. It was a new dynamic for us. I declined his offer, so instead, he held my arm and slowed his pace to match my heavy, Braxton-Hicks-laden steps. We made it home. Just a couple weeks after that, he met his grandson.

Two pregnancies later, the Missing took to walking a couple of paces in front of me to show off its bright white tennis shoes as we took our daily trudge to the mailbox. It led the way. Self-assured in its identity as the presence that took the place of my kids' grandpa. I resented its energetic gait.

When Bria Grace entered the world, filling the room with her healthy screams, the Missing once again stepped forward for its turn to hold the baby. Again, it cradled her swaddled form, slowly rocked back and forth, back and forth, and sang its favorite song,

*"If only, if only, if only..."*

This time, I knew the plaintive tune well. With longing flooding my spirit, I hummed along.

## QUESTIONS AMONG THE ROOTS

I took Lyla on a pilgrimage to her grandpa's gravesite—just me, her, and the roots. She's grown into a sentimental and thoughtful child. I watched her skip between rows of stone on the soft, hollow, hallowed ground.

Somehow, she made skipping look reverent and respectful. The Missing stood to the side observing. Its gait had slowed. It seemed as though the rushing prairie winds had pushed back against it enough to keep it contained. It was more observer than wild dervish on this particular visit to the gravesite. It watched Lyla with a half smile. She is irresistible even to the Missing.

On another summer visit to Winnipeg, Dad laid out the turquoise striped picnic blanket that had accompanied us on many family outings. I think we'd picked it up in New Mexico on one of our many road trips through the desert. He stretched out on the blanket, laid on his back, and allowed a not-yet-walking Jude to crawl around him and over him. The best grandpas turn into jungle gyms.

It was the same blanket I now spread out atop Dad's grave, soggy from a recent rain shower. I lay on my belly and stretched out the full length of where Dad's casket had been—poised above frozen ground before Clarence lowered it. The cracks in the earth beckoned me to peer down into them to catch a glimpse of— *what?* There was nothing to see.

I wanted to remember the grandpa who had lain on the ground to be close to his grandson. The grandpa who let his grandson slobber all over his black framed glasses.

The Missing stretched out on its stomach with me. The blanket is the link between what had been and what should be. More grandchildren should have had the chance to climb over their grandpa's laughing belly. Like the grandchild who now reverently skipped over honeycomb earth.

Unable to read as of yet, Lyla picked out letters and sounds she recognized on the headstones. The Mennonite surnames. She was unaware of the many connections made between them in the limbs of our family tree—*her* family tree.

She asked too many questions. I say *'too many'* because she even shocked the Missing with the graphic nature of her curiosity. *Were they all buried in their boxes? Were they facing up or down? Which way do their heads point? But what do they look like, Mom?*

I tried to meet her with the same lighthearted childishness with which the questions were posed, but some of the questions brought back the trauma of the day I first stood around that cold rectangle stamped out of the frozen ground.

I didn't want to think about my daddy in the ground in any manner of decomposition. I didn't want to remember the still, waxen skin and the suit jacket Mom and I had chosen specifically to be buried forever among the entangled roots. Alas, my imagination is as untamed as the Missing once was.

There are times I want to close my ears to the questions—to seal the memory of Dad up in its pine box and leave it there. I could reduce his memory to merely being a name or picture on a family tree or granite stone. But I know questions are good. Questions are vital. Questions are healthy. Being receptive to the questions of the living gives way to the introduction of those that have passed on. No, I can't just leave him in his box to become merely a name on a stone. I want to try to introduce my children to who their grandpa was. Though I will miss the mark, I will keep trying to explain the unexplainable. I will keep trying to respond to the questions knowing full well the inevitable insufficiency of any answer I can come up with. Getting comfortable with questions is a step toward peace.

Grief is a question that hangs in the air.

It just lingers—hovering there like the last word hurled in a vicious argument before a storm out and a door slam. It's the kind of silence that still speaks volumes; it can't quite be called quiet because there's no resolution. There is only emotion, pain, anger, confusion, and the words you *should have, could have* said.

You're left floating in a sort of emotional purgatory—waiting for a satisfying answer to the question—and your only companion in the waiting room is the Missing.

I wonder sometimes if someday I will get to Heaven and have an argument with God. Maybe *'argument'* is the wrong word. It will be more like an inquisition. I'll circle around God's throne like the bad cop, grilling Him for answers. Then again, maybe I will be awestruck into peaceful submission by His holiness. Maybe seeing Dad again will be enough of an answer.

Maybe presence is the answer to grief.

*They* say time cures all things. I think it's likely that rather than time, it is actually presence that is the cure. Whether it is the presence of my departed dad or experiencing the presence of an answer-giving Goodness. When the presence of the Missing will once again be exchanged in a final answer, the question mark will be turned into a period—resolution will be found through reunion.

While there is hope in that, there is also the awareness that there is no cure for grief, for the grieving aren't sick. Just as the cures for cancer, though they advance daily, are sporadic and unreliable, the cure for grief—or at least the colicky, violent, fresh grief—is perhaps an adjustment to the wilderness of questions. When we can grow accustomed to the persistent questioning tone, and the rise in pitch at the end of a sentence, the Missing will stop feeling cruel and become more of a companion than an antagonist.

Leaving the graveyard that day, the Missing sat in the back seat with Lyla, tapping its white tennis shoes just a little offbeat to the song on the radio and humming along. We drove away from the precious granite rock, back across the fields of Manitoba. Lyla's youthful face was thoughtful, eyes catching the green from the rushing stripes of soybeans alternating with canola yellow from outside her window.

"I wish Grandpa Fred didn't have to die. I hate cancer. Can I say I hate cancer?"

She's been taught to use the word *'hate'* with discretion.

That answer was easy. "Yes, you can hate cancer."

I can't be angry with God about Dad dying. I mean I can, but I choose not to stay there too long. Oh, I have raged at Him. He has borne the brunt of my ugly emotions. I would be a fool to try to temper myself with the All-Knowing, to hold back what is real just because it is painful or unattractive. He already knows me entirely, so to fake it is pointless. I can rage at Him, but I will not alienate Him. It was cancer that broke Dad. Cancer. Not

God. I will not give up on God in response to losing Dad. That feels rebellious against who Dad was.

And I have learned in this topsy-turvy world God set deliberately on a tilt spinning and orbiting through space, I need my Abba.

I need Him in the disorienting dizziness. I need Him in the loneliness. I need Him when the Missing assumes its full strength and when my husband is gone for long amounts of time. I need Him with every stark reminder of my fallible humanity. I need Him when fear creeps in and when worry squeezes tight. I need Him when the world is on fire and I can't catch my breath.

When I find myself railing at the swirling winds and throwing flying fists against the thunder of the Missing and when the infinite number of tearful questions have congealed into one big one, I wait. I wait with anticipation. I wait for the scarred palm to hold my cheek. Then, I can finally breathe out

*Abba, I belong to You.*

Then, I can catch a heavenly glimpse of Dad leaning over to his best friend Jesus, punching Him playfully on the arm and chuckling at his grandkids.

And although he has long since entered the presence of perfect answers, I think Dad also knows he is missing out. I think he resents the Missing a little. I think he wishes he could be here to play hide-and-seek and teach Jude how to use the screwdriver he'd given him.

Maybe Heaven doesn't take the missing and the longing away. Maybe missing and longing simply cease to be uncomfortable or painful.

For now, the Missing and I set up camp in the wilderness of unending questions, like a curious 6-year-old rapidly firing them off machine gun style—the embodiment of innocent curiosity. In this wilderness, I make my home where the questions far outnumber the answers.

When I lean my cheek against the duck feather softness of my littlest's head, she gives in to sleep, contentedly unaware yet what she is missing out on and the robbery she has been born into. Palm on cheek, cheek on sleepy head—the Missing humming and pacing the hall in its white tennis shoes—always there. The questions hang in the air above us—humming along, buzzing, and open-ended—but I'm getting used to them.

As I'm getting used to the Missing.

———————————

*One day I awoke and began my day. I plodded mechanically down the hall to the coffee pot.*

*My sleep had been void-like. The Missing hadn't made an appearance.*

*It felt like a severing. A dropped call—when you keep talking without realizing you're babbling to no one. Where had the Missing gone? I sought it out. I needed to know where it was.*

*In a sickening realization of Stockholm syndrome, I found that instead of the relief I had been longing for, I felt panic.*

*What if it had left me, and with its leaving, took away the memories? What if the leaving of the Missing was a new sort of taking, a loss of connection, a distancing—a distancing I didn't want. Frantic, I called for it.*

*It was immediately at my side, and to my dismay, I yelped in relief.*

*As painful as the Missing was, I wasn't ready for the drifting away into the distance.*

*After that, the Missing began to save its appearances for significant days on the calendar. Days on which it would launch itself onto my shoulders causing me to stumble around under its full weight. On those days, the bruises felt fresh although they were fading.*

*In a twisted turn of events, I began to anticipate the times when it would stay close to me. I even looked forward to it. Its presence once again was heavy and painful, closing the distance in between.*

*With an exaggerated bow, the Missing gives me permission to feel. The feelings rise to the surface. The Missing assumes its full expanse.*

*Then it shrinks down again. Manageable. Willing to stay in its room.*

## CHAPTER 10

# The Legacy of the Missing

Bria has started pointing at the moon which will always make me think of Dad. The moon takes me back to that night when it shone so brightly above the funeral home. And takes me further back still to a grandpa teaching his grandson what to look for.

She is keenly aware of it, noticing it in the daytime, as well as on the rare occasions she's awake to see it aglow in the night sky. The other day she asked me why the moon was "cracked in half." It took me half a second to decipher she was referring to the crescent shape. She is beginning to understand the phases and that the moon looks different from day to day and night to night.

When grief moved in, I too was *cracked in half.* But grief, much like the moon, changes phases. It can wax and wane; it can be both ferocious and heartbreakingly tender. It tells us when to harvest and pushes and pulls the tide. It casts its silvery light across *everything.*

When the Missing entered my life, it changed the way I viewed and interacted with the world around me. Many things for me are now filtered through the lens of grief. I see it every-where— all the ways in which the Missing manifests in other people's worlds besides my own.

Sometimes my familiarity with the Missing has made me better at showing up for people who are grieving. I am generally aware of what stupid things *not* to say because they were said to me. I can wrap them in a soft blanket of empathy. When I say, "I understand, "I really do. The Missing becomes a tether binding us together. And it is also this connection that has the potential of keeping us from being swept away. We need to find other grievers in the world, other people who know the Missing.

And yet other times, I find I'm worse at showing up for others in their grief. I run. The memory of lilies and formaldehyde paralyzes me into inaction. In all honesty, sometimes the trauma of my own experiences causes me to instinctively pull away from other people's pain rather than join them in it. Simply put, I know too much now. I know the brutality of a lifetime of robberies. I know the burial of the *before*, planted deep into honeycomb earth, lined with stone.

Yet, even though it hurts, there are times I've decided I must "*keep the wound from healing,*" as Nicholas Wolsterstorff says in his book "Lament for a Son." I "shall try to *keep the wound from healing in solidarity with those who sit beside me on humanity's mourning bench.*"[4] It is, therefore, a conscious and intentional choice I've had to make to dive into another's pain and join them there along with the Missing.

Much like the changing phases of the silver moon, with time, the Missing has lost much of its sharp ferocity and violent power. Now, it is more of a dull, persistent ache that never seems to let up. This *'waning'* has brought with it a pain and a grief I never anticipated.

With each passing year, I feel further away from his memory. As the Missing loses its sharp edges in the tossing of the waves, a sadness in me rises that Dad is further in my past. The distance settles in. In the grip of fresh grief, the memories of Dad were easier to see. Now, I find it more challenging to conjure up his scent or recall the sound of his voice, whereas before it dropped into my mind with regular ease.

Sometimes I worry that in my grief and his absence, I idealize Dad and my childhood in a way that isn't entirely accurate.

I find myself second-guessing my own mind. I have accepted that I am a woman with so-called *'Daddy issues'*. You can't lose a father such as mine and not acquire them. Perhaps I've set Dad up on an impossible pedestal. I have a tendency to don rose-colored, gilded-edged glasses and observe the world around me through them.

Dad was human, after all. He was far from perfect, and along with all of the things that made Dad remarkable and wonderful, I also have to be intentional about recognizing the other things I know to be true about him:

- Sometimes his preacher side beat out his listener side.
- Sometimes the ministry came before his family.
- Sometimes our safety and emotional well-being played second fiddle to the *'calling'*.
- There were elements of *'colonialism'* and *'white saviorism'* in his ministry that perhaps unintentionally caused harm.
- He didn't know how to rest.
- At times he mistook arrogance for confidence.
- Sometimes he said yes to us when it should have been no, and no when it should have been yes.
- When we asked for guidance, he would inevitably respond, "well, what are you called to?" This is an ambiguous question—not easily answered and often unhelpful.
- Sometimes the line between faith and denial blurred together.
- His ice cream portion sizes were obscene.

His weaknesses were all of these and likely more. Yet, while I never want to set him up as infallible or perfect, he was *my* dad. And a lot of who I am is wrapped up in who he was. *All* that he was. And his influence knows no bounds, for, in many ways, I can only now understand and appreciate my true identity through the filter of losing him and adjusting to life with the Missing. Just as the sky would be bereft without the presence of the silver moon, I have come to realize that grief is now an irrevocable part of who I am.

## PYRAMIDS

There are lines of ants that march the trails leading to the Mayan ruins of Tikal in Guatemala. I saw them. All in an endless line at my feet, one after another, like a tiny caravan.

When I took a closer look, I could see they were carrying bits of green leaf ten times the size of their own bodies. Still, they marched on. It looked as though the leaves were alive themselves, but really it was the minuscule laborers doing the heavy lifting.

I know without a doubt God gives us more than we can handle. We can count on it. It's not that He is the source of grief or pain because in Him there cannot be darkness. He is love, and He is light, and He is all the way *good*. Still, to say He doesn't give us more than we can handle is simply not true. Life, in and of itself, is already far more than we can handle.

Yet, even when I've found myself sprawled out in agony on my kitchen floor, rendered powerless against the onslaught of the Missing brought on by a mere song that dared to play, even as I lay belly to the ground, stretched out in the Niverville cemetery, yearning to feel the nearness of my father—even then, we steady on.

Somehow, we wake up the next morning with a fresh set of mercies. Somehow, we keep marching forward, bearing the weight of our experience and trauma. Heavy laden, we plod on-ward.

I tried not to think of snakes and large insects as my family and I, in our own line, mimicked the ants' march. One foot in front of the other, we journeyed into the Guatemalan jungle. My hot pink fanny pack, buckled around my waist, jingled with each step. I kept pace behind Dad, following him into the thick, green foliage. Spider monkeys leaped from branch to branch in the canopy high above us. *Were they mocking us or cheering us on?* We couldn't even see our destination through the woven tapestry of exotic plants.

"That's a pyramid," our guide said, pointing his machete at a tall hill completely covered in moss and plants. Entire trees were growing out of this alleged *'pyramid'*.

I'd hoped that wasn't what we'd hiked for an hour to see—a pre-excavated pyramid still covered up by dirt. This was not what I expected.

We continued on, parallel to the line of ants. Finally, the enormous jungle parted, and we stepped out into a green clearing and into the uncovered Mayan city of Tikal. The tallest pyramid, the *Jaguar,* rose high above the rest of its subjects—regal and impressive. The air around me was humid and hot, not unlike Georgia air, and teeming with supernatural energy. The hairs on my arms stood up as if responding to an invisible latex balloon. I was fully aware of the ancient roots beneath my feet.

The mighty *Jaguar* had once itself been just a cone-shaped mound of earth —tucked in and sleeping—camouflaged by dirt and trees. Its former glory was buried deep. Dormant, it wait-ed until someone began to dig it up, removing the blanket of years, revealing the steps that lead to the skies. Steps that allow a person—even an 11-year-old girl—to stand higher than spider monkeys.

Standing atop the *Jaguar* was scary and intimidating. I'm not a huge fan of heights, but I am a big fan of awe and wonder, and this moment was full of it. I was acutely aware of my own smallness, and yet I was lifted high. For that moment, I was in a place of honor. I felt unbelievably significant simply because of the expansive view I was privy to.

Grief is like that now. I'm finally up where I can see. With the wind in my face, the air is easier to breathe.

It's been nearly a decade since the Missing moved in and buried me. These past few years have felt like an uncovering, an exhuming of the remains of my former life. *What is left now that I have come up for air?* I can see these dark years laid out behind me. I see where I was and where I am now.

I am also well aware that it is here, at the top of the pyramids, where the sacrifices took place. And there have been many, many times in this grief journey where I have felt completely gutted and spilled out. I've questioned God, *"Is it worth it?"* And yet, I don't think God works that way. Although God wastes not one drop of sacrificial blood or salty tears, He is not the one with the knife in His hand.

The Missing is still a bully. It shows up loud and proud every year on March 22nd to scratch another tally mark into my skin. It shows up again on May 26th to blow out imaginary candles with dragon breath. On Father's Day, it hangs out with feigned casualness— just waiting to be acknowledged.

Though it can still be malicious, it is no longer the monster it once was. In fact, it's a great storyteller. It talks to me about who I am and who my father was. It speaks prophetic words over my children. It tells of what they have the capacity to be and the inheritance into which they have been born.

The Missing is with me as I climb every laborious step on stairs of ancient stone too narrow for my feet. It puts its hand in mine so I can feel its calluses. Its fingernails are round and brown with soil from the digging—the pulling up of spidery roots. White New Balance sneakers lead the way. Up, up, and up some more—sure-footed and secure. It knows where it's going.

The Missing puts its hand on my shoulder to steady me on these heights and helps me take in the view from the top. From the perch of my new vantage point, I can see it all. Well, maybe not *all,* but enough. Enough that I'm not suffocating anymore by the unknowns and the unseens. I am now walking in the land of '*and yet*'.

I suffered, *and yet*—

I sacrificed, *and yet*—

I vehemently reject the notion of our pain always having a purpose.

Sometimes wrenching redemption out of our pain dishonors it. We are not meant to be the Redeemer. Still, I can see where my pain was not wasted. I can see where the life-altering decisions C.J and I made have brought about tremendous good for our family and how we are healthier because of them.

I like the independence that has grown in me as a result of learning what loneliness feels like. I've surprised myself with what I am capable of. I see my children struggling with hard emotions, and yet they are already capable of great empathy because they know what '*hard*' feels like.

I've learned how to sprawl out in my king-sized bed when my husband is away. The Missing is crowded to the very edge while I sleep like a proud starfish, who only multiplies when split apart.

I often think back to the young mother sending her husband off for the first time into the military world. I remember the fear. The shadows. The crushing weight of responsibility. I have sacrificed—and yet. Now, with three deployments under my belt and countless orders issuing him to be far away, C.J. and

I have learned to appreciate one another with a greater depth that comes from sacrifice and missing one another.

And perhaps it's okay for a member of the armed forces to have a spouse who clings to her pacifism and brings it up regularly in conversation. Perhaps a certain level of holy tension is a good thing. Just maybe the whole point is to ask the questions not necessarily to receive satisfactory answers but because there is value in the mere asking.

From this vantage point, I can see where parts of me have been unearthed and uncovered. I have risen tall above my circumstances, and I've grown. Now, I can look out over the leafy, green canopy carpet where spider monkeys play—unrolled into the vast expanse of my past and present. I'm finally able to step back from the blur of minuscule dots and brush strokes to take in the big picture. And though I will resent the Missing for what it took from me until the day I cash it in for all of the glorious answers to my collection of questions, the fear of heights is wearing off, and I can finally take in the view.

## A DAUGHTER'S SONG

Shortly after Dad died, I dreamed of him.

In the dream we were walking and talking; he was in his white tennis shoes. After a while, he turned to me and asked,

*"How did it happen?"*

His own death had taken him by surprise. I did my best to relay the details of his last days. He was thoughtful as he pondered and processed his own death, but peaceful.

Together we walked to a wooden shelf. It was an outdated, golden oak shelf with a curved top that one might find hanging on the wall of an antique store. On it sat an assortment of coffee mugs, lined up in eclectic rows. He scanned the shelf with his green eyes for a few seconds before selecting a mug and placing it in my hands. On its porcelain side was written one word: *Sing*.

He wrapped his arms around me. For a brief second, I felt the bristles of his mustache on my cheek before I awoke, my eyelids full of captive tears.

If there is anything I believe deep in my bones, it's that this world is capable of tremendous beauty, even beauty that comes out of pain. Dad was one of the best at loving people as they were and believing vehemently that God's grace extends to all.

One of Dad's last mentees was a man named Timothy. Timothy was a sex offender. That was his label and his conviction.

Timothy called from prison the week after Dad died. I listened as Mom told Timothy that Dad was gone. I could hear his uncontrolled sobbing on the other end of the line from where I sat in the other room. By all earthly standards, Timothy was abandoned. He was locked up in a system with little hope for rehabilitation. Up until then, Timothy phoned my parents' house just about every day, and now Dad would no longer be there to take his calls. The Missing moved in for Timothy that day, too.

Dad believed until his last breath there is no such thing as lost causes. Though he understood it should never cover consequences or accountability, he believed that no one is beyond hope. Not even Timothy.

Perhaps it's this steadfast belief that led to us being completely ill-prepared for his funeral because Dad died still believing in the impossible.

Dad's occupation in life as a "Servant to All" included getting to know as many people as possible to more fully understand their stories. Toward the end of his life, I believe his view of God was wider and more complete because he hoarded a lifetime of stories from others and walked alongside them. Stories are sacred. Stories carry the capacity for transformation.

My dad moved through the world alert and locked in on his identity. After he died, we found an entry in his journal, written just before the Missing would begin its robbery:

*"What is my focus? It cannot be about what I am doing now. Things change so quickly in my world. It's not about what I should now do though I see needs all around me. It's not about what I want to do to somehow change others. No, my identity is based on what God my Father already did in sending His only Son for the world to see what He has done for the whole world but also just for me. My identity is in Jesus. Let the cross always be the center point and nothing else. May I find my full identity in Him and Him alone. May it be in the power of the cross that I find my identity. He can heal. He has my future in His hands. He can re-shape those whom I love and care for."*

On my journey to honor my father's memory, then, it is abundantly clear that loving others in the name of Jesus is how I will do so, especially those who are hard to love and whom the world would quickly deem *'lost causes.'* I will teach my children to love as their grandpa did—with reckless abandon.

I will not forget the poor. I will always consider those who are marginalized. I will fight for peace in this dissonant world. I will chase adventure and embrace cultures unlike my own. I will work to give grace and forgiveness reflexively. I will look the homeless in the eye and learn their names. I will stand guard against those who seek to strip the image of God from *any* human being on this planet. We all bear God's face—just as I bear my dad's legacy.

---

The Missing shows up in many forms. I can see how the Missing for me, now very much resembles my dad, but there are other *'Missings'* in my life that have moved in. In this life, I've realized I am constantly missing someone or something. I miss my childhood. I miss my family. I miss the smell of home and our California lemon tree. I miss how it felt to fall in love and then the joy of being a bride. I miss cooking for two and the youthful awkwardness of the teenagers we ministered to. I miss the prairies and the power of the thunderstorms. Yes, I even miss the scent of tornados. I miss the smell of my firstborn's baby head and the way he pronounced helicopter *"hepatopter."* I miss the sound of Lyla's toddler voice and her gloriously curly hair framing her heartbreakingly green eyes. I miss Bria's squishy thighs that have stretched long as she's grown out of her babyhood.

There's always something to miss—to long for. To look back on and wish we'd really taken it in when we were in it. Yet, the longer I live with the persistent missing, the more I grow to understand: The Missing will only be at rest when it is found in the presence of Abba. An Abba that never leaves nor forsakes. Even as I write these familiar Biblical words, I hear the voice of Dad in my head. I hear the inflection he used when reading me a bedtime story. I hear the rise and fall in pitch as he reaches the end of the story, finally trailing off in the last word. I hear the same vibrating gentle growl in the back of my own throat when I finish the last page of my daughter's bedtime story.

This is the echo of legacy. This is where the continuation of his pastorship happens. It lives on in the echoes of those whose lives his own merged with. It lives on in my children. It lives on in me.

And, so, I must *'sing'*.

I must open my mouth, allow beauty to come out of it.

I *must* tell his story.

Even if that means I must allow the Missing to have a voice in mine.

*Abba, I belong to You.*

---

*The Missing's violent episodes have become fewer. I no longer flinch from its touch or hide from its presence. Curiously and gradually, it seems to have gotten baptized by the waters of time.*

*There was a fade. As if a divine hand turned the dial to the left on the Missing's ferocity and cruelty.*

*Its touch, once so malicious, turned gentle—repentant even. Apologetic. Rather than pull me into pain, it began to reveal small redemptions. Its forceful presence has turned into a coaxing. A beckoning. It draws me closer.*

*The projections above my bed play in soft focus. The realism has faded. I don't know that I trust what I see. At times I feel the truth has been manipulated into rosy idealism. Still, I stare at them. I am a moth to their flame. They are irresistible.*

*The sharp edges of the pain have grown round and smooth from the relentless tumbling in the Missing's waves.*

*Rather than the stench of death and dying, the Missing now trails wafts of motor oil, fresh cut grass, and soap.*

*In moments of sadness, I have even found The Missing to be comforting. I lean into it, the side of my head making soft contact with a t-shirt-clad shoulder. It holds my cheek with a gentle, calloused hand and whispers, "Remember."*

*I still resent its presence and wish it had never come. I wish it had stayed far far away from me. Curiously though, it seems to want to atone for its initial violence.*

*The marks on my wrists have faded to small, silver crescent moons.
I stroke them with my thumb, remembering the sting.*

*The Missing has taken its leave and confined itself to its room.
There, it will live out the rest of our days. We will grow old together.
It peeks its head out when it wants to show me something.*

*On occasion, I turn the knob and open the door to its room, seeking
out its company. We sit on the floor cross-legged and turn the pages
of memory books. Journals with scribbled words. Photos. Birthday
cards. It keeps a playlist going, filling the room with the sounds
of the past. It projects memories that are less images or events and
more so impressions and feelings.*

*It brings me popcorn on a tray and a bowl piled high with rocky
road ice cream.*

*Its presence seems to be summoned by my emotions. Whether I am
overcome with joy and gratitude or stressed and overwhelmed—it is
then that it is once again at my side, buzzing with energy.*

*When the pain of life and brutality of this world bangs on the
windows and doors, the Missing takes firm hold of my wrist. It
points its aging finger at the moon—round fingernails dark with
car grease and soil.*

*The Missing is no longer a presence of evil or pain, but rather an
abstraction of who is missing.*

*Would that I could trade the Missing for the real thing.*

*I pull on its hem when I want a story. When I want to remember
what was lost. When I want to feel young again.*

*The Missing tells the best stories.*

*Clinging to its hem, I find it is unraveling as I hold onto it.*

*It is spinning into a gossamer thread—the color of moonlight on breaking waves—and I see it stretches across endless waters.*

*I pull hand over hand. I draw myself forward across this salty, tear-filled ocean. Despite the waves still rolling, my feet don't sink. I fix my eyes on the golden horizon and move onward.*

*I know with every day and every hand over hand—I get a little closer to the end. To the end of the waves. The end of the endless.*

*The end of the Missing.*

1. Brennan Manning, *The Furious Longing of God,* (Colorado Springs, CO: David C. Cook, 2009), 46.

2. C.S. Lewis, *A Grief Observed,* (Great Britain: Faber & Faber, 1961), 21.

3. Brennan Manning, *The Furious Longing of God,* (Colorado Springs, CO: David C. Cook, 2009), 55.

4. Nicholas Wolterstorff, *Lament for a Son,* (Grand Rapids, MI: Eerdmans, 1987), 63.

# Acknowledgements

It is hard to believe this book finally exists. The loneliness of an author's life was not something I was entirely prepared for. This book was written in the never-by-myself stage of motherhood. The majority of the words in these pages came into being with a child on my lap or in the room.

The village that came around me at different points along the way is precious and varied.

My friends and family who have cheered me on and spoken words of encouragement when the doubts were loud and the courage was timid, you have no idea how much I needed you. Especially those of you who know the Missing well but read my roughest drafts anyway. You know who you are. Reading this work is in many ways pushing on the bruise of your grief. Your empathy and "I thought I was the only one" made me believe this could be a book worth reading.

To Justin and Hayley, still, the most convenient thing to ever happen to me. Thank you for being there for me in countless ways and for being the wise and generous people you are.

To the team at Lucid Books, thank you for being my compass through this overwhelming publishing wilderness.

To Jeff Crosby, my industry expert, and friend. Thank you for believing in me. Without your gentle and encouraging feedback, I doubt this book would have happened. I probably would have given up. Having you in my corner made every difference.

For Vicki, my shining Scottish knight with her red pen. Thank you for allowing me to lay this jumbled ball of knots before you. You untangled it with kindness, grace, and brilliant skill.

To C.J., my best friend, and love of my life. Thank you for holding me up and allowing me to be unabashedly myself, even when it means bearing my soul and sharing our story. You love me when I am at my best and at my worst, and I love you for that.

And Mom, the most adventurous soul I know. Your faith and courage are a formidable force in the face of mediocrity. You have never stopped praying for me, believing in this book, and loving me. Dad would be so proud of his bride.